Jacques Cartier, Samuel de Champlain
and the Explorers of Canada

General Editor

William H. Goetzmann
Jack S. Blanton, Sr., Chair in History
   University of Texas at Austin

Consulting Editor

Tom D. Crouch
Chairman, Department of Aeronautics
   National Air and Space Museum
   Smithsonian Institution

WORLD EXPLORERS

Jacques Cartier, Samuel de Champlain
and the Explorers of Canada

Tony Coulter

Introductory Essay by Michael Collins

CHELSEA HOUSE PUBLISHERS

New York • Philadelphia

On the cover Map of Canada by Samuel de Champlain; portraits of Samuel de Champlain and Jacques Cartier

Chelsea House Publishers
Editor-in-Chief Richard S. Papale
Managing Editor Karyn Gullen Browne
Copy Chief Philip Koslow
Picture Editor Adrian G. Allen
Art Director Nora Wertz
Manufacturing Director Gerald Levine
Systems Manager Lindsey Ottman
Productions Coordinator Marie Claire Cebrián-Ume

World Explorers
Senior Editor Sean Dolan

Staff for JACQUES CARTIER, SAMUEL DE CHAMPLAIN, AND THE EXPLORERS OF CANADA
Copy Editor Margaret Dornfeld
Editorial Assistant Robert Kimball Green
Picture Researcher Patricia Burns
Senior Designer Basia Niemczyc

7 9 8 6

Library of Congress Cataloging-in-Publication Data

Coulter, Tony
Jacques Cartier, Samuel de Champlain, and the explorers of Canada/Tony Coulter: introductory essay by Michael Collins.
p. cm.—(World Explorers)
Includes bibliographical references and index.
Summary: Surveys the early exploration of Canada by Cartier, Champlain, and others.
ISBN 0-7910-1298-0
    0-7910-1521-1 (pbk.)
1. Canada—Discovery and exploration—French—Juvenile literature. 2. Canada—History—To 1763 (New France)—Juvenile literature. 3. Explorers—Canada—History—Juvenile literature. [1. America—Discovery and exploration—French. 2. Canada—History—To 1763 (New France) 3. Cartier, Jacques, 1491–1557. 4. Champlain, Samuel de, 1567–1635. 5. Explorers.]
I. Title. II. Series.   92-14159
F1030.C812 1992   CIP
971.01'13—dc20   AC

CONTENTS

WORLD EXPLORERS

THE EARLY EXPLORERS

Herodotus and the Explorers of the Classical Age
Marco Polo and the Medieval Explorers
The Viking Explorers

THE FIRST GREAT AGE OF DISCOVERY

Jacques Cartier, Samuel de Champlain, and the Explorers of Canada
Christopher Columbus and the First Voyages to the New World
From Coronado to Escalante: The Explorers of the Spanish Southwest
Hernando de Soto and the Explorers of the American South
Sir Francis Drake and the Struggle for an Ocean Empire
Vasco da Gama and the Portuguese Explorers
La Salle and the Explorers of the Mississippi
Ferdinand Magellan and the Discovery of the World Ocean
Pizarro, Orellana, and the Exploration of the Amazon
The Search for the Northwest Passage
Giovanni da Verrazano and the Explorers of the Atlantic Coast

THE SECOND GREAT AGE OF DISCOVERY

Roald Amundsen and the Quest for the South Pole
Daniel Boone and the Opening of the Ohio Country
Captain James Cook and the Explorers of the Pacific
The Explorers of Alaska
John Charles Frémont and the Great Western Reconnaissance
Alexander von Humboldt, Colossus of Exploration
Lewis and Clark and the Route to the Pacific
Alexander Mackenzie and the Explorers of Canada
Robert Peary and the Quest for the North Pole
Zebulon Pike and the Explorers of the American Southwest
John Wesley Powell and the Great Surveys of the American West
Jedediah Smith and the Mountain Men of the American West
Henry Stanley and the European Explorers of Africa
Lt. Charles Wilkes and the Great U.S. Exploring Expedition

THE THIRD GREAT AGE OF DISCOVERY

Apollo to the Moon
The Explorers of the Undersea World
The First Men in Space
The Mission to Mars and Beyond
Probing Deep Space

CHELSEA HOUSE PUBLISHERS

Into the Unknown

Michael Collins

It is difficult to define most eras in history with any precision, but not so the space age. On October 4, 1957, it burst on us with little warning when the Soviet Union launched *Sputnik*, a 184-pound cannonball that circled the globe once every 96 minutes. Less than 4 years later, the Soviets followed this first primitive satellite with the flight of Yury Gagarin, a 27-year-old fighter pilot who became the first human to orbit the earth. The Soviet Union's success prompted President John F. Kennedy to decide that the United States should "land a man on the moon and return him safely to earth" before the end of the 1960s. We now had not only a space age but a space race.

I was born in 1930, exactly the right time to allow me to participate in Project Apollo, as the U.S. lunar program came to be known. As a young man growing up, I often found myself too young to do the things I wanted—or suddenly too old, as if someone had turned a switch at midnight. But for Apollo, 1930 was the perfect year to be born, and I was very lucky. In 1966 I enjoyed circling the earth for three days, and in 1969 I flew to the moon and laughed at the sight of the tiny earth, which I could cover with my thumbnail.

How the early explorers would have loved the view from space! With one glance Christopher Columbus could have plotted his course and reassured his crew that the world was indeed round. In 90 minutes Magellan could have looked down at every port of call in the *Victoria*'s three-year circumnavigation of the globe. Given a chance to map their route from orbit, Lewis and Clark could have told President Jefferson that there was no easy Northwest Passage but that a continent of exquisite diversity awaited their scrutiny.

In a physical sense, we have already gone to most places that we can. That is not to say that there are not new adventures awaiting us in the sea or on the red plains of Mars, but more important than reaching new places will be understanding those we have already visited. There are vital gaps in our understanding of how our planet works as an ecosystem and how our planet fits into the infinite order of the universe. The next great age may well be the age of assimilation, in which we use microscope and telescope to evaluate what we have discovered and put that knowledge to use. The adventure of being first to reach may be replaced by the satisfaction of being first to grasp. Surely that is a form of exploration as vital to our well-being, and perhaps even survival, as the distinction of being the first to explore a specific geographical area.

The explorers whose stories are told in the books of this series did not just sail perilous seas, scale rugged mountains, traverse blistering deserts, dive to the depths of the ocean, or land on the moon. Their voyages and expeditions were journeys of mind as much as of time and distance, through which they—and all of mankind—were able to reach a greater understanding of our universe. That challenge remains, for all of us. The imperative is to see, to understand, to develop knowledge that others can use, to help nurture this planet that sustains us all. Perhaps being born in 1975 will be as lucky for a new generation of explorer as being born in 1930 was for Neil Armstrong, Buzz Aldrin, and Mike Collins.

The Reader's Journey

William H. Goetzmann

This volume is one of a series that takes us with the great explorers of the ages on bold journeys over the oceans and the continents and into outer space. As we travel along with these imaginative and creative journeyers, we share their adventures and their knowledge. We also get a glimpse of that mysterious and inextinguishable fire that burned in the breast of men such as Magellan and Columbus—the fire that has propelled all those throughout the ages who have been driven to leave behind family and friends for a voyage into the unknown.

No one has satisfactorily explained the urge to explore, the drive to go to the "back of beyond." It is certain that it has been present in man almost since he began walking erect and first ventured across the African savannas. Sparks from that same fire fueled the transoceanic explorers of the Ice Age, who led their people across the vast plain that formed a land bridge between Asia and North America, and the astronauts and scientists who determined that man must reach the moon.

Besides an element of adventure, all exploration involves an element of mystery. We must not confuse exploration with discovery. Exploration is a purposeful human activity—a search for something. Discovery may be the end result of that search; it may also be an accident, as when Columbus found a whole new world while searching for the Indies. Often, the explorer may not even realize the full significance of what he has discovered, as was the case with Columbus. Exploration, on the other hand, is the product of a cultural or individual curiosity; it is a unique process that has enabled mankind to know and understand the world's oceans, continents, and polar regions. It is at the heart of scientific thinking. One of its most significant aspects is that it teaches people to ask the right questions; by doing so, it forces us to reevaluate what we think we know and understand. Thus knowledge progresses, and we are driven constantly to a new awareness and appreciation of the universe in all its infinite variety.

The motivation for exploration is not always pure. In his fascination with the new, man often forgets that others have been there before him. For example, the popular notion of the discovery of America overlooks the complex Indian civilizations that had existed there for thousands of years before the arrival of Europeans. Man's desire for conquest, riches, and fame is often linked inextricably with his quest for the unknown, but a story that touches so closely on the human essence must of necessity treat war as well as peace, avarice with generosity, both pride and humility, frailty and greatness. The story of exploration is above all a story of humanity and of man's understanding of his place in the universe.

The WORLD EXPLORERS series has been divided into four sections. The first treats the explorers of the ancient world, the Viking explorers of the 9th through the 11th centuries, and Marco Polo and the medieval explorers. The rest of the series is divided into three great ages of exploration. The first is the era of Columbus and Magellan: the period spanning the 15th and 16th centuries, which saw the discovery and exploration of the New World and the world ocean. The second might be called the age of science and imperialism, the era made possible by the scientific advances of the 17th century, which witnessed the discovery of the world's last two undiscovered continents, Australia and Antarctica, the mapping of all the continents and oceans, and the establishment of colonies all over the world. The third great age refers to the most ambitious quests of the 20th century—the probing of space and of the ocean's depths.

As we reach out into the darkness of outer space and other galaxies, we come to better understand how our ancestors confronted *oecumene*, or the vast earthly unknown. We learn once again the meaning of an unknown 18th-century sea captain's advice to navigators:

> And if by chance you make a landfall on the shores of another sea in a far country inhabited by savages and barbarians, remember you this: the greatest danger and the surest hope lies not with fires and arrows but in the quicksilver hearts of men.

At its core, exploration is a series of moral dramas. But it is these dramas, involving new lands, new people, and exotic ecosystems of staggering beauty, that make the explorers' stories not only moral tales but also some of the greatest adventure stories ever recorded. They represent the process of learning in its most expansive and vivid forms. We see that real life, past and present, transcends even the adventures of the starship *Enterprise*.

A New World for France

Although it would eventually come to claim the better part of North America, France was the last major seafaring power of Europe to take a significant interest in the New World. While, beginning in the 1490s, Spanish sailors and Portuguese mariners were discovering and conquering the islands of the Caribbean and the lands of Central and South America, and England was sending out searchers for the Northwest Passage, France's interest in the mysterious regions being discovered across the ocean to the west was limited to trips made by Breton (a native of the region of Brittany) fishermen to the Grand Banks, an exceptionally rich fishery off the island of Newfoundland. As fishermen, then as now, were not wont to boast about choice locations, little is known about these first French voyages to the New World, in which, in any event, France's government, preoccupied with wars and intrigue in Italy, took little official interest.

That state of affairs began to change in 1524, when King Francis I of France sent Giovanni da Verrazano, a Tuscan noble by birth and "a well educated, imaginative, and aggressive seaman" (the words of historian Lawrence Wroth), in search of a northwest passage to Asia. Though Verrazano failed in his stated objective—for the simple reason that no such passage exists at the latitudes where he was looking—he did explore the North American coastline from the Carolinas as far north as Nova Scotia. In so doing, he did more than any European explorer of his

The Breton mariner Jacques Cartier, European discoverer of the St. Lawrence River, is often portrayed as looking somewhat gloomy and introspective, with a dark, forked beard and a piercing gaze. This is more artistic convention than history, however, for no portraits of Cartier from his lifetime exist.

day to demonstrate that an unknown northern continent, not just a number of islands or an outcropping of Asia, lay to the west across the ocean, but he was unable to convince Francis of the value of establishing colonies along the rich coastline he had explored.

Francis's interest in the New World lay dormant until 1532—the king was, wrote the great American historian Francis Parkman, "always ardent at the outset of an enterprise and always flagging before its close"—when he made a pilgrimage to the island abbey of Mont-Saint-Michel, in southern Normandy. There, one of the country's most powerful clergymen, Jean Le Veneur, abbot of Mont-Saint-Michel, bishop of Lisieux, and grand almoner of France, introduced him to one Jacques Cartier, a relative of the abbey's bursar. Le Veneur assured Francis that "by virtue of his voyages to Brazil and the New Land," Cartier

This detail from a 16th-century French tapestry shows Portuguese caravels setting off on voyages of exploration. By sending its bold mariners on voyages along the west coast of Africa and then around the Cape of Good Hope, Portugal, more than any other European nation, initiated the new age of exploration that culminated in the New World voyages of the late 15th and early 16th centuries.

was the ideal man "to lead ships in the discovery of new territories in the New World." The cleric even went so far as to promise that "if the King would consent to entrust this mission to Jacques Cartier . . . [he would] provide chaplains and contribute to the cost of these voyages of discovery from his own resources." Still hopeful of discovering a direct route to Asia, and of perhaps establishing a vast empire, the king agreed, and Cartier was duly commissioned to make the great voyage.

Little is known of Cartier's personal or professional life before his meeting with Francis I. The man who would stake France's claim to the St. Lawrence Valley, the seat of its New World empire, was born to Jamet Cartier and

A Theodore de Bry engraving, dated 1562, of the bustling commerce along the Lisbon wharf. In the 15th and 16th centuries, Portugal's and Spain's discoveries of new lands to plunder and trade with made them the richest nations of Europe.

Among those who allegedly beat the French to the New World was the 6th-century Irish monk St. Brendan, who was said to have sailed the Atlantic in a small, open fishing boat called a currach. At one point, as depicted in this 17th-century French engraving, Brendan supposedly landed on an uncharted isle and said Mass, only to discover that the isle was in fact the back of a huge whale. Tales of fantastic creatures would become a staple of the exploration literature of the New World.

Geseline Jansart in Saint-Malo, a port town in the seafaring region of Brittany that "had been for centuries a nursery of hardy mariners," according to Parkman, sometime between June 7 and December 23 of 1491. In the civil register in which his marriage to Marie Katherine des Granches was recorded in 1519, he is described as a "master-pilot"; by 1532, according to Le Veneur, he had made trips to Brazil and the "New Land [Newfoundland]." In Saint-Malo, whose sailing men had long been visiting Newfoundland to fish, he had a reputation as a solid navigator, an excellent commander, and a just leader of men. Nothing more is known. He is usually portrayed as dark-haired, bearded, and with a gloomy or thoughtful countenance.

The objective of his expedition, according to the royal order issued for payment of the cost of his equipment, was to "voyage to that realm of the *Terres Neufves* [New World] to discover certain isles and countries where it is said there must be great quantities of gold and other riches." From the narrative of the expedition itself that is usually attributed to Cartier, it seems that he understood his commission more specifically to be a search for a northwest passage to the Orient via, according to another royal document, the "baye de Chasteaux," or Bay of Castles. (Although solid historical evidence indicates that Cartier may not have been the actual author of the existing narratives of his three journeys, they are usually attributed to him nonetheless, primarily because the writer based his account on Cartier's logbooks.) The Bay of Castles was in fact the channel known today as the Strait of Belle Isle, which runs for 90 miles between the northern tip of the island of Newfoundland and southeast Labrador and connects the Atlantic Ocean with the Gulf of St. Lawrence. The misnomer by which French cartographers then referred to it—that is, as a bay rather than a strait—indicates the dearth of information available to Cartier about the regions he intended to explore.

Giovanni da Verrazano was entrusted by King Francis I with France's first New World venture, which was inspired by the king's jealousy of the wealth accruing to his Iberian rivals as a result of their overseas explorations. Verrazano (pictured) was probably a member of the lesser Tuscan nobility, though he may have been born in the French city of Lyons, which was then home to a large Italian community.

A 1586 woodcut of Saint-Malo, Cartier's birthplace. According to the American historian Francis Parkman, the foremost chronicler of France's New World ventures, Saint-Malo was "an ancient town . . . thrust out like a buttress into the sea, strange and grim of aspect, breathing war from its walls and battlements of ragged stone, a stronghold of privateers, the home of a race whose intractable and defiant independence neither time nor change has subdued."

Cartier sailed from Saint-Malo on April 20, 1534, with two ships of around 60 tons each and a combined crew of 61 men. (Neither the names of the ships nor the identity of anyone who sailed with Cartier on that first voyage are known.) Extremely favorable weather allowed the vessels to make the ocean crossing in exceptional time; his ships reached Cape Bonavista, on the eastern coast of New-foundland at about the same latitude as Saint-Malo, on May 10, and the Bay of Castles a little more than two weeks later.

En route, they stopped at a small islet, well known to French mariners as L'Isle des Ouaisseaulx (the Isle of Birds). Thirty-two miles northeast of Cape Freers, the tiny, rocky island was the nesting ground of tens of thousands of birds, foremost among them the great auk, a clumsy, flightless, penguinlike creature, and the gannet, which according to Cartier "bit even like dogs" when their nests were disturbed. Even so, in half an hour Cartier's men were able to slaughter two boatloads' worth of the island's fowl, to be used as food at some later time. While sailing northwest from the island, Cartier and his men spied a swimming polar bear, "as big as a cow and as white as a swan." The men took to the ships' boats and killed the snowy bruin, whose meat they found "as good and delicate to eat as that of a two-year-old steer."

Icebergs and foggy weather prevented Cartier from beginning his navigation of the Strait of Belle Isle until June 9, at which time his two ships began sailing west along the coast of Labrador, exploring various harbors, islands, and bays, including one known as Les Islettes (present-day Bradore Harbor), where, Cartier noted, "much fishing" was carried on by European vessels. Confirmation of this statement came several days later in the Gulf of St. Lawrence, along the coast of the present-day province of Quebec, where at Shecatica Bay the explorers met a large fishing ship from the French city of La Rochelle. It accompanied Cartier's vessels as far west as present-day Cumberland Harbor, which Cartier originally named after himself and declared "one of the best [harbors] in the world." His admiration for the roadstead stood in sharp contrast to his regard for the rest of the land he had seen thus far. This, he felt, "should not be called the New Land, being composed of stones and horrible rugged rocks; for along the whole of the north shore [of the Gulf], I did not see one cart-load of earth. . . . I am rather inclined to believe that this is the land God gave to Cain."

At about this time, Cartier had his first encounter with Native Americans, probably Beothuks, whose habit of painting their bodies, clothing, and belongings with red ocher may have given rise to the phrase "red Indian."

Though Europeans almost unanimously described the Beothuks as "inhuman and wild," there is no indication that their initial reception of Europeans was hostile. Cartier said of the people he saw along the north shore of the gulf:

> [Their] bodies are fairly well formed but they are wild and savage folk. They wear their hair tied up on the top of their heads like a handful of twisted hay, with a nail or something of the sort passed through the middle, and into it they weave a few bird's feathers. They clothe themselves with the fur of animals, both men as well as women; but the women are wrapped up more closely and snuggly in their furs; and have a belt about their waists. They [all] paint themselves with certain tan colours. They have canoes made of birch-bark in which they go about, and from which they catch many seals.

On June 15, Cartier's two ships began sailing across the gulf toward the western coast of Newfoundland, a course that put them in completely uncharted waters. On reaching Newfoundland, Cartier explored south along the coast for 10 days, naming the many capes and harbors he encountered, then set a westward course once again. By so doing, he failed to discover Cabot Strait, which separates Newfoundland and Cape Breton Island, although heavy tides did lead him to suspect the existence of "a passage between Newfoundland and the Breton's land." In the gulf, the mariners came upon three islands "as completely covered with birds . . . as a field is covered with grass." They called these stony rookeries, where they killed thousands of wildfowl, the Isles de Margaulx; they are known today as the Bird Rocks. Some ten miles west, almost in the center of the gulf, they found a beautiful island, about four miles long and one mile wide, that Cartier named Brion. Brion Island was, Cartier asserted, "the best land we have seen; for two acres of it are worth more than the whole of Newfoundland. We found it to be covered with fine trees and meadows, fields of wild oats, and of pease in flower, as thick and as fine as ever I saw in Brittany. . . . There are numerous gooseberry bushes, strawberry vines. . .[and] roses, as well as parsley and other useful, strong-smelling herbs." It was also home to a strange animal unknown to the Frenchmen, "great beasts like large oxen, which have two tusks in their jaw like elephant's tusks and swim about in the water." The walruses easily eluded the sailor's efforts to capture them.

Brion Island's preeminence in the explorer's eyes was soon eclipsed by Prince Edward Island, which the mariners first sighted on June 30. Cartier assumed it to be part of the mainland; it was, he wrote, "the finest land one can see, and full of beautiful trees and meadows." On one of the four excursions made to the island—Cartier was especially in-terested in examining its forests—the French caught sight of an Indian who "ran after our long-boats along the coast, making frequent signs to us. . . . [W]e began to row towards him, but when he saw that we were returning, he started to run away. . . . We landed opposite to him and placed a knife and a woolen girdle on a branch; and then returned to our ships," in which they set sail toward the eastern coast of what is known today as New Brunswick, where they landed at Escuminac Point.

Now heading north, Cartier made a careful examination of the New Brunswick coast. On July 3, he located "a large bay and opening" stretching due west, bordered on the north by hilly, forested country. Hopeful that this apparent-ly unlimited expanse of water was the Northwest Passage itself or a route to it, Cartier was deeply disappointed when subsequent investigation proved his "strait" to be a bay, which he named the Baie de Chaleur (Bay of Heat) because of the warmer climate that seemed to prevail there.

In the course of their exploration of the bay, Cartier and his men would become the first Frenchmen in recorded history to have a significant encounter with the native peoples of North America. On July 6, while exploring in a

This 17th-century French en-graving shows Indians hunting wildfowl on the rocky islet Cartier named L'Isle des Ouaisseaulx (the Isle of Birds). "These is-lands," according to Cartier, "were as completely covered with birds, which nest there, as a field is covered with grass." Later ex-plorers reported that the Indians who called there in birch-bark canoes did not even have to use clubs to kill fowl; they simply trampled the birds to death.

longboat, a party of Frenchman saw "fleets of Indian canoes that were crossing from one side [Baie de Chaleur] to the other, which numbered in all some forty or fifty canoes." Undiscouraged by warning fire from Cartier's cannons, the Indians—who were Micmacs—expressed with gestures their desire to trade with the newcomers, "dancing and showing many signs of joy, and of their desire to be friends."

The following day, nine Micmac canoes called on the French ships at St. Martin's Cove, where they lay at anchor. The Indians once again

> made signs to us that they had come to barter with us; and held up some furs of small value, with which they clothe themselves. We likewise made signs to them that we wished them no harm, and sent two men on shore, to offer them some knives and other iron goods, and a red cap to give to their chief. Seeing this, they sent on shore part of their people with some of their furs; and the two parties traded together. The savages showed a marvellously great pleasure in possessing and obtaining these iron wares and other commodities, dancing and going through many ceremonies, and throwing salt water over their heads with their hands.

Another cultural and material exchange took place on the bay's north shore during Cartier's return voyage from its head. Attracted by fires lit on the beach near present-day Tracadigash Point by some Micmacs, the explorers took their longboats to the entrance to the lagoon, where they were soon approached by several of the Indians, who offered them strips of cooked seal meat. Two of the Frenchmen then went ashore with hatchets, knives, beads, and other items, in which the Micmacs "showed great pleasure." A crowd of Indians quickly formed, numbering

> both men, women and children, more than 300 persons. Some of their women . . . danced and sang, standing in the water up to their knees. The other women . . . advanced freely towards us and rubbed our arms with their hands. Then they joined their hands

together and raised them to heaven, exhibiting many
signs of joy. And so much at ease did the savages feel
in our presence, that at length we bartered with them,
hand to hand, for everything they possessed, so that
nothing was left to them but their naked bodies; for
they offered us everything they owned, which was,
all told, of little value.

After several days of northward travel, Cartier was compelled by stormy weather to anchor his ships in the Baie de Gaspé. On the shores of this "good and safe harbor," a group of more than 300 Indians appeared, come to fish for mackerel. These were so-called Canadian Iroquois, most likely descendants of Mohawks who had migrated northeast three centuries earlier. By language and culture they were linked with a nation of tribes whose influence and domain extended over most of the eastern woodlands of present-day Canada and the United States.

  Though the Iroquois nation would play a central role in the history of Canada until nearly the end of the 18th century, Cartier, the first European to establish relations with them, was not overly impressed by his first encounter:

> This people may well be called savage; for they are the
> sorriest folk there can be in the world, and the whole
> lot of them has not anything above the value of five
> sous, their canoes and fishing-nets excepted. They go
> quite naked, except for a small skin, with which they
> cover their privy parts, and for a few old furs which
> they throw over their shoulders. . . . They have their
> heads shaved all around in circles, except for a tuft
> on the top of their head, which they leave long like a
> horse's tail. This they do up upon their heads and tie
> in a knot with leather thongs. They have no other
> dwelling but their canoes, which they turn upside
> down and sleep on the ground underneath.

At their first meeting, the French gave the Iroquois glass beads, combs, knives, and other small trinkets, at which "they showed many signs of joy, lifting up their hands to

Cartier named one of the more comely islands he discovered on his first voyage after Philippe de Chabot, seigneur de Brion, who was the admiral of France and his most enthusiastic supporter at Francis's court.

The title page of the first French edition of the narrative of Cartier's first voyage, which appeared in 1596. Editions had already been published in Italian, in 1556, and in English, in 1580 and 1582, perhaps indicating the lack of interest in New World exploration in France.

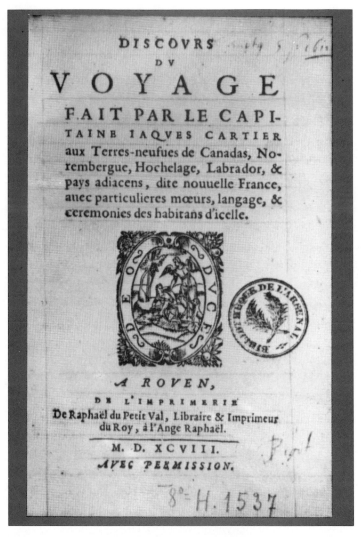

DISCOVRS
D V
VOYAGE
FAIT PAR LE CAPI-
TAINE IAQVES CARTIER
aux Terres-neufues de Canadas, No-
rembergue, Hochelage, Labrador, &
pays adiacens, dite nouuelle France,
auec particulieres mœurs, langage, &
ceremonies des habitans d'icelle.

A ROVEN,
DE L'IMPRIMERIE
De Raphaël du Petit Val, Libraire & Imprimeur
du Roy, à l'Ange Raphaël.
M. D. XCVIII.
AVEC PERMISSION.

heaven and singing and dancing in their canoes." On July 22, the French rowed from their ships in longboats to the Iroquois encampment, where the Europeans' offerings of combs and tin bells and rings induced much merriment, especially among the Indian women, "who crowded about [Cartier] and rubbed him with their hands, which is their way of showing welcome." Two days later, Cartier had a 30-foot cross erected at the mouth of Gaspé harbor. The cross bore a shield with three fleurs-de-lis, the symbol of

France's monarchs, beneath a wooden plaque on which was carved in large letters the legend VIVE LE ROY DE FRANCE (Long live the king of France.) The French had staked their first claim to the New World.

The significance of the ceremony was not lost on the Iroquois. Soon after the cross was raised, according to Cartier,

> the chief, dressed in an old black bear-skin, arrived in a canoe with three of his sons and his brother. . . . [P]ointing to the cross he made us a long harangue, making the sign of the cross with two of his fingers; and then he pointed to the land all around about, as if he wished to say that all this region belonged to him, and that we ought not to have set up this cross without his permission.

Gifts and flummery disarmed the chief, whose name was Donnaconna. The French showered the chief with presents and assured him that the cross was nothing more than a guidepost to ensure their safe return. Donnaconna, who had reasons of his own for securing the friendship of the newcomers, eventually decided to allow two of his sons to sail with them back to France.

Cartier's ships left the Bay of Gaspé on July 25. Hampered by fog, they sailed initially to the northeast, by virtue of which they reached the southeasternmost point of Anticosti Island, which Cartier took to be a peninsula of the mainland. Once the ships rounded a point that Cartier named Cap Saint-Louis (present-day East Cape), open water stretched ahead of them to the northwest. Cartier took his ships into this passage, which he named the Strait of St. Pierre, but strong winds and currents stymied their progress. On August 1, he called together "all our Captains, Masters, and Mariners" to sound their advice on what should be done next. In consideration of the lateness of the season, "that we were even now very far [from home] and knew not what dangers lay ahead," it was decided, "almost unanimously," to return to France.

Searching
for Saguenay

Though Cartier had failed to discover either a route to China or "great quantities of gold and other riches," his voyage to the Gulf of St. Lawrence had nonetheless been fruitful enough to interest Francis I in a follow-up expedition. The Strait of St. Pierre had been only half-explored and might yet reveal itself as a passage to Asia or other fabulous lands; new territory, some of it fertile and abundant in wildlife, had been discovered, along with new peoples, most of them friendly and eager to trade; and Francis, envious of the vast overseas empire claimed by his great rival, King Charles V of Spain, was eager to expand France's holdings. Domagaya and Taignoagny, the two Iroquois whom Cartier had brought back to France, spoke of a great river that flowed through their territory and of a kingdom called "Saguenay," rich in copper and other valuables.

Thus it was that by October 30, less than two months after his return—his ships had landed at Saint-Malo on September 5, 1534—Cartier had received a royal commission to complete his "navigation in the lands beyond the *Terres Neufves* whose discovery you have already begun." To do so, he was given "power and special command" over three ships and some 110 men. Cartier himself was to sail aboard *La Grande Hermine* (the Great Ermine), which was twice the size of either of his ships on the first voyage, as captain and pilot; accompanying the flagship were to be *La*

Meeting of the potentates: King Francis I of France exchanges pleasantries with Charles V of Spain. At the height of his power, Charles ruled over present-day Spain, the Netherlands, Belgium, Luxembourg, Austria, Mexico, Naples, Sicily, and much of Germany and South and Central America, a dominion whose extent Francis could only aspire to.

An artist's conception of La Grande Hermine, *Cartier's flagship on his second voyage to the New World. The ship carried 12 guns and was about 120 tons burden. Among the approximately 110 men who sailed with Cartier on the second voyage were 7 carpenters, a barber-surgeon, an apothecary, and a trumpeter.*

Petite Hermine (the Small Ermine) and *L'Emerillon* (the Sparrowhawk). This last vessel was a pinnace, a small ship, perhaps 40 tons, equipped with both sails and oars, that was better suited than the larger vessels for coastal exploration. Of the crew, 12 were Cartier's kinsmen, including the captain of *La Petite Hermine.*

The tiny fleet left Saint-Malo on May 19, 1535. It enjoyed good weather for a week, at which time the ocean "turned bad and stormy and continued so for such a long time with incessant headwinds and overcast sky that no ships that have crossed the ocean ever had more of it." The tempests prevailed for a month, eventually separating the vessels on June 25. Cartier's ship made Funk Island on July 7, some fifty days after leaving Saint-Malo, then proceeded to the western end of the Strait of Belle Isle, where it anchored and awaited its two companion vessels, which arrived on July 26.

Cartier's main objective was to reach the northwestern end of the gulf in order to resume his investigations of the Strait of St. Pierre. Accordingly, he made no extensive investigations of the Quebec coast as he took his fleet westward. At Anticosti, at least one of his geographical misconceptions was cleared up when he learned from Domagaya and Taignoagny that that particular body of land was in fact an island; the peninsula was "Honguedo," the land to the southwest where Cartier had erected the cross. (Honguedo is known today as the Gaspé Peninsula.) From Honguedo, said the Indians, lay the route to the Indian kingdom of "Canada"—a name here making its first appearance in the historical record. Two days' journey from Anticosti, they claimed, "began the kingdom of the Saguenay, on the north shore as one made one's way towards this Canada."

After a cursory reconnaissance of Honguedo and its superb forests—"as excellent for making masts for ships of three hundred tons and more as it is possible to find"—Cartier took his ships across the gulf again to explore the Quebec coastline near the entrance to the St. Lawrence River. This region, Domagaya and Taignoagny asserted, was

> the beginning of the Saguenay and of the inhabited region . . . thence came the copper they called *caignetdaze*. . . . The two Indians assured us that this was the way to the mouth of the great river of Hochelaga and the route towards Canada, and that the river grew narrower as one approached Canada; and also that farther up, the water became fresh, and that one could make one's way so far up the river that they had never heard of anyone reaching the head of it.

On September 1, the French flotilla entered the St. Lawrence River and began sailing the "route towards Canada." The ships moved slowly now, fearful of running aground, and Cartier sometimes took them in circles so as to examine both banks of the river. An abundance of wildlife—especially beluga whales, "with head like a greyhound . . . none of us remembers seeing so many," and walruses, "fish in appearance like horses which go on land at night but in the daytime remain in the water"—attracted their notice. Some 20 miles upstream, the expedition came upon a "deep and rapid" river that "issued from between lofty mountains of bare rock with but little soil upon them" and flowed into the St. Lawrence from the northwest; this was, according to Domagaya and Taignoagny, the "route to the kingdom and country of the Saguenay." While surveying the mouth of the Saguenay, Cartier and his men encountered a group of Iroquois who had come from Canada in four canoes to fish and hunt for seals. The Indians regarded the French ships with "great fear and trembling," but when the lone canoe that dared approach came close enough for Domagaya and Taignoagny to identify themselves—they were dressed in European clothes—the Indians were greatly reassured and came alongside Cartier's vessels "in all confidence." Six days later and farther upstream, Cartier's ships reached a group of 15 islands; the

This extract from the "original ledgers of the savings accounts," dated March 1535, authorizes the payment of 6,000 livres (a unit of French currency) to Cartier so that he may "discover certain islands where it is said that there must be great quantities of gold and of other precious things."

archipelago, according to their Indian guides, marked "the point where the province and territory of Canada begins."

The largest of the islands—some 21 miles long and 7 miles wide—Cartier initially named Bacchus, for the abundance of grapes that grew there, but he later reconsidered and renamed it Ile d'Orleans, after the third son of Francis I. Ashore, he and his men encountered a party of Iroquois, who were overjoyed to recognize Domagaya and Taignoagny. According to Cartier, the Indians began

dancing and going through many ceremonies. And some of the headmen came to our long-boats, bringing us many eels and other fish, with two or three measures of Indian corn, which is their bread in that country, and many large melons. And during that day many canoes filled with the people of the country, both men as well as women, came to our ships to welcome our two Indians.

Drawn in the 1600s by a later French explorer of the region and one of the first historians of New France, Marc Lescarbot, this map of the St. Lawrence region shows the lands visited by Cartier in the course of his explorations.

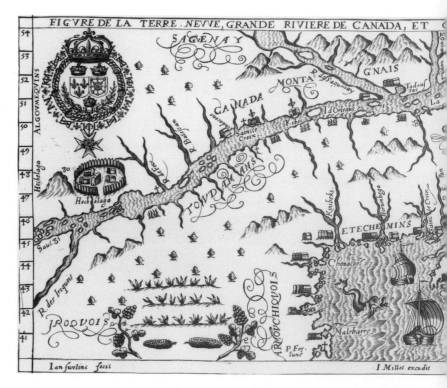

The following day brought the "lord of Canada" himself, Donnaconna, with a suite of 12 canoes, to the French vessels. As he drew near *L'Emerillon*, Donnaconna began "to make a speech and to harangue us, moving his body and his limbs in a marvellous manner, as is their custom when showing joy and contentment," Cartier wrote. When their father boarded Cartier's vessel, Domagaya and Taignoagny began telling him "what they had seen in France and the good treatment meted out to them there. At this the chief was much pleased and begged the captain to stretch out his arms to him that he might hug and kiss them, which is the way they welcome one in that country." Cartier then offered the Iroquois some bread and wine, and after a short celebration the Frenchmen continued upriver, passing en route beneath a majestic stone promontory (known to history as the Rock of Quebec) near which, on a "double ridge of land, at a good height and cultivated all about,"

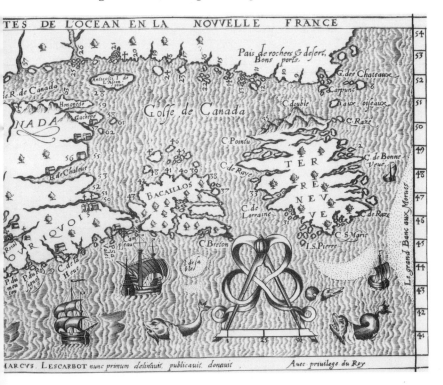

An artist's romanticized conception of the arrival of Cartier and the French in early September 1535 near the Indian village of Stadacona, not far from the future site of the city of Quebec.

stood Donnaconna's village, Stadacona. The surrounding countryside, according to the Cartier narrative, was "as fine land as it is possible to see, being very fertile and covered with magnificent trees of the same varieties as in France." Cartier had his ships lay in at a safe anchorage nearby.

Though they maintained an outward friendliness, the Indians at Stadacona were wary of their French visitors— the explorers were never invited to the village itself, for example—and their mistrust seemed to be justified when they learned that Cartier intended to proceed even farther upriver, to Hochelaga, an even larger settlement at the site of present-day Montreal. Cartier may have styled Donnaconna the "lord of Canada," but it was the Indians at Hochelaga—also Canadian Iroquois but probably Onondaga rather than Mohawk in origin—who dominated the entire St. Lawrence Valley. A canny potentate, Donnaconna wished to cement an alliance with the French that would allow his people to become the most powerful in the region, and he was determined not to allow the French to establish a relationship with his enemies at Hochelaga.

But cajolery and dissimulation—the river was "not worth exploring" farther up, the French were told—failed to dissuade Cartier, and so, too, did Donnaconna's offer of three children, including his young niece, in exchange for a promise to go no farther. (Such an offer indicates the importance, to Donnaconna and his people, of the alliance they were proposing; by giving the Frenchmen their children, they were essentially making symbolic kinsmen of the Europeans.) Though willing to take the children, who would serve as hostages to ensure the continued friendliness of the Stadacona natives, Cartier insisted that he would go to Hochelaga nevertheless, whereupon Donnaconna gave him the children as a gesture of goodwill. In return, Cartier honored the chief with a gift of two swords and two brass chamber pots.

To celebrate their agreement, Donnaconna asked Cartier to fire a salute from his ships' guns. His sons had told him impressive tales about the power of these cannons, but the Iroquois were unprepared for the full effect of a 12-gun salvo. As the cannonballs crashed into the woods opposite, the Indians "were all so much astonished as if the heavens had fallen upon them, and began to howl and shriek in such a very loud manner that one would have thought hell had emptied itself there." The Indians then claimed that two of them had been killed by the barrage, perhaps hoping that

One of the primary sources of information about Cartier's last two voyages is the writings of André Thevet, a seagoing monk and self-styled cosmographer who spent five months as Cartier's houseguest after the Breton's exploring days were over.

thereby, by dint of remorse, the French would be convinced to stay with them, but Cartier was unmoved.

Cartier's stubbornness angered Donnaconna and his gods. On the following day, September 18, a canoe bearing three Indians appeared in the water near the French ships. This trio was "dressed up . . . as devils, array[ed] . . . in black and white dog-skins, with horns as long as one's arm and their faces coloured black as coal." As the canoe passed by the French ships, the "devils" averted their faces, and on reaching the shore they fell to the bottom of their vessel like

This 1565 engraving by de Bry shows American Indians worshiping the Devil. The first French explorers of the New World had little doubt that Lucifer and his minions inhabited the thick forests of North America, and one of the most prevalent New World myths concerned the so-called Isle of Demons. "I myself have heard it," wrote Thevet, "not from one but from a great number of the sailors . . . that when they passed this way they heard in the air . . . a great clamor of voices . . . whereupon they well knew the Isle of Demons was not far off."

dead men. Waiting villagers quickly seized the canoe and carried it into the woods.

A little while later, Taignoagny and Domagaya appeared, acting greatly astonished. Lifting his eyes toward heaven, Taignoagny proclaimed, "Jesus, Jesus, Jesus," while his brother, also gazing skyward, called out the names of Jesus, Mary, and Jacques Cartier. When Cartier asked what the trouble was, they replied that their god, whom they called Cudouagny, had made an announcement, which had been transmitted to the tribe by the three devils the French had seen earlier: There would be so much ice and snow at Hochelaga that Cartier and his entire party would perish should they go there. Scornfully, Cartier informed the Iroquois that Cudouagny was a fool and that Jesus would protect them from the cold. The next day, Cartier, with 50 sailors and all his officers, departed for Hochelaga in *L'Emerillon* and two longboats. The rest of the men stayed behind with the two larger ships.

The French were greatly impressed by the land they now passed through. On both sides of the river, according to the Cartier narrative, was "the finest and most beautiful land it is possible to see . . . as level as a pond and covered with the most magnificent trees in the world." The banks were also covered with grapevines, and "the sailors came back on board with their arms full of [grapes]." Cartier was amazed by the huge number and variety of birds that made their home in the forest; he listed "cranes, swans, bustards, geese, ducks, larks, pheasants, partridges, blackbirds, thrushes, turtle doves, goldfinches, canaries, linnets, nightingales, sparrows, and other birds." Though he was mistaken in some of his identifications, the St. Lawrence Valley was then home to an astonishing abundance of wildlife.

It was populated as well by a significant number of human inhabitants, and the French saw many huts along the banks of the river. Their residents "came towards our boats in as friendly and familiar a manner as if we had been natives of

European readers of New World travel narratives were most fascinated by the descriptions of the native inhabitants of the recently discovered continents. This illustration appeared in Thevet's Les Singularitéz de la France Antarctique, *which was published in 1557. Unlike the Spanish, the French did not refer to Native Americans as Indians: Their most common term was* sauvages *(savages).*

the country, bringing us great stores of fish and of whatever else they possessed, in order to obtain our wares, stretching their hands towards heaven and making many gestures and signs of joy."

Some 32 miles upriver from Quebec, Cartier and his men reached a spot known today as Portneuf, which lies opposite Platon Point at the foot of the Richelieu rapids. Near where they dropped anchor, they soon discovered, lay the village of Achelacy (also known as Hochelay), whose chief soon arrived with several canoes to greet the newcomers. Farther up, the river grew extremely difficult to navigate, he warned the French, and they should not trust Donnaconna and his two sons, who were treacherous. He then gave Cartier his nine-year-old daughter.

The Achelacy chief's words regarding the difficulty of navigation soon proved accurate, as rapids and narrow channels slowed the explorers' progress to a little better than eight miles a day. On September 28, the French reached Lac Saint-Pierre, a widening of the St. Lawrence to 20 miles at the end of which a number of small islands divides the river into five channels. On one of the islands, the explorers met a party of five Indians who were hunting muskrats. The Indians, wrote Cartier, "came to meet our boats without fear or alarm, and in as familiar a manner as if they had seen us all their lives. And when our long-boats grounded, one of these Indians took the Captain in his arms and carried him on shore as easily as if he had been a six-year-old child, so big and strong was that Indian." A conversation conducted in signs yielded the information that Hochelaga was three days' journey upriver.

At this point, out of concern for the lateness of the season, Cartier decided not to take *L'Emerillon* any farther. With 32 men, he continued on in the two longboats. Three days and 45 miles later, they reached Hochelaga, on the island known today as Montreal, where they were greeted by more than a thousand people, who gave them, according to the Cartier narrative, "as good a welcome as ever father gave to his son."

Situated near a mountain and surrounded by cornfields, Hochelaga was a more typical Iroquois settlement than Stadacona. It was entirely surrounded by a circular wooden stockade; above the single fortified gate, and at many points around the enclosure, were galleries where great piles of rocks, to be used as weapons of defense in case of a siege, were stored. Within these fortifications stood some 50 large wooden houses, arranged in neat rows. The houses were divided into many separate rooms; in the middle of each was a large open space without a floor, where fires were lit.

The newcomers were received like gods at Hochelaga. Upon their arrival in the open square at the center of the village, a large group of weeping women and girls, some of them carrying babies, crowded around them and implored the explorers to touch their children. The men of the village then sat down in a circle around the French, as if, wrote the author of the Cartier narrative, "we had been going to perform a miracle play." Ten Iroquois then entered the square, carrying the paralyzed chief of the village on a large deerskin. At his direction, Cartier rubbed the chief's arms and legs with his hands; satisfied, the chief doffed his red crown of porcupine quills and presented it to the explorer. At once a crowd of sick, blind, and lame Indians were brought in for Cartier to lay his hands on. It was as if, according to Cartier, the Iroquois at Hochelaga believed "Christ had come down to earth to heal them." Cartier then read aloud several passages from the Bible, distributed various trinkets, and ordered his men—much to the delight of the Indians, who showered them with cornbread—to sound trumpets and other musical instruments.

The French then set out to explore the nearby mountain, which Cartier named Mont Royal (known today as Montreal). From its summit Cartier could see the forested landscape, with mountains to the east, west, and south, for many miles around and trace the course of the St. Lawrence "as far as the eye can reach." Upstream, clearly visible, was a boiling stretch of rough water, "the most impetuous one can see." Given the sarcastic name La Chine (China) by a French explorer of the next century, René-Robert Cavelier, sieur de La Salle, who was also seeking a passage to the Orient, these rapids dropped 42 feet in two miles and were for many years to constitute an impassable barrier to further European navigation of the St. Lawrence.

The Hochelaga Iroquois then informed the French that another large river, which ran from the west like the St. Lawrence, flowed through the mountains to the north (the Laurentides). This was the Ottawa River, which Cartier at once suspected might be the river that led to the kingdom of Saguenay. Without any prompting, the Indians took hold of a silver chain worn by Cartier and the gilt handle of a sailor's copper dagger and indicated that gold and silver could be found in a kingdom up the Ottawa ruled by a warlike people they called the Agojuda, or bad people, who carried many weapons and wore armor made of plates of wood bound together with cord.

Though certainly intrigued by these reports, Cartier recognized that it was too late in the season to begin further

exploration, and he took his men back to the longboats, then immediately set off downriver, followed for some distance by a flotilla of Indian canoes. He reached *L'Emerillon* on October 4, and the French set sail for Canada the next day. Except for a brief stop to explore the mouth of the St. Maurice River, their progress downstream was uninterrupted, and they returned to Stadacona on October 11.

Cartier's trip to Hochelaga had made for uneasy relations between the men he left behind and the residents of

Cartier left no visual portrayals of the native inhabitants of the St. Lawrence Valley whom he encountered. Samuel de Champlain, who in the next century founded the colony of New France in the regions discovered by Cartier, made these drawings of some of the native peoples he found there.

The branches of a tree Cartier called the annedda were the crucial ingredient in the antiscorbutic potion that enabled his expedition to survive its winter at Stadacona. The Indians "brought back from the forest nine or ten branches and showed us how to grind the bark and boil it in water, then drink the potion every other day and apply the residue as a poultice to swollen and infected legs," Cartier wrote. He believed that all the most educated doctors in Europe "could not have done as much in a year as this tree did in a week."

Stadacona. Feeling threatened, his men had built a fort near where their ships were anchored, made of large logs planted upright and tied together and guarded with artillery, but Donnaconna professed to be overjoyed by Cartier's return and extended a formal invitation for the Frenchman to visit him at the village.

Accompanied by 50 armed sailors, Cartier paid his first visit to Stadacona on October 13. According to the cosmographer André Thevet, who later questioned Cartier at length about the expedition, the houses the French saw there were "made in the fashion of a semi-circle, twenty or thirty paces long, ten in width, some covered with the bark of trees, others with sea rushes." During the course of the visit, Donnaconna, eager to demonstrate the fighting prowess of his people, showed Cartier the scalps of five Indians, "stretched on hoops like parchment," that belonged to "Toudamans from the south [probably Micmacs or Etchemins], who waged war continually against his people." The chief described a brutal surprise attack the Toudamans had made on his people some time back and vowed to Cartier that he would have vengeance.

Relations between the French and the Indians deteriorated further over the next few weeks. Taignoagny and Domagaya informed their compatriots that the French had been taking advantage of them by trading worthless trinkets for valuable supplies, and the Indians were further angered by Cartier's refusal to return the three children Donnaconna had given him. Fearful of attack, and now committed by virtue of the lateness of the season to wintering in Canada, Cartier gave orders to strengthen the fort by surrounding it with a moat and adding a gate and drawbridge. He also directed that four nightly watches be kept, with a fanfare of trumpets announcing the changing of the guard.

But cold weather and disease, not the Indians, proved to be the explorers' greatest enemies. From mid-November through mid-April their ships were locked in ice more than 12 feet thick, while on shore 4 feet of snow piled up. "All our beverages froze in their casks," Cartier recorded, "and on board our ships, below hatches as on deck, lay four fingers' breadth of ice."

Of even greater danger than the cold was the "pestilence"—scurvy—that broke out among the explorers and the Indians in mid-December. The initial symptoms of scurvy, which is caused by a lack of vitamin C in the diet, are bleeding gums, loosening teeth, and pain in the joints; left untreated, it progresses to internal bleeding and hemorrhaging, acute physical weakness, the opening of scar tissue, severe weight loss, apathy, depression, dementia, and death. By mid-February, 25 of the Frenchmen had died and 50 seemed near death; no more than 10 of the original 110, among them Cartier, were untouched by the disease. The corpses of the dead were "buried" in snowdrifts. Though Cartier feared that knowledge of the weakened state of the French expedition would prompt the Indians to launch an attack—whenever some Indians approached the fort, he ordered his few able-bodied men to create a tremendous racket of banging and hammering so that the Indians, who were never allowed inside, would be deceived into thinking that the entire party was hard at work—the residents of Stadacona were themselves suffering terribly from the disease, to which at least 50 of them succumbed.

Domagaya provided the remedy; he told Cartier that the juice and pulp of the leaves of a tree he called *annedda*— probably *Thuya occidentalis* (white cedar), whose leaves are rich in vitamin C—cured his particular case of the ailment. At first, Cartier's men refused to even sample the concoction, but those who overcame their initial revulsion quickly "recovered health and strength and were cured of all the diseases they ever had." Soon, all the men were clamoring for the potion, and some of them even claimed that the libation cured their syphilis.

The Indians also touted the therapeutic benefits of another native North American plant—tobacco, which they smoked in long narrow pipes with the stem in front rather than on top. Cartier wrote:

> At frequent intervals they crumble this plant into pow-
> der, which they place in one of the openings of a hol-
> low instrument, and laying a live coal on top, suck at
> the other end to such an extent, that they fill their
> bodies so full of smoke, that it streams out of their
> mouths and nostrils as from a chimney. They say it
> keeps them warm and in good health, and never go
> about without these things. We made a trial of this
> smoke. When it is in one's mouth, one would think
> one had taken peppered powder, it is so hot.

The residents of Stadacona provided additional geographic information as well. They told Cartier that the Ottawa River "flows through two or three large, very broad lakes, until one reaches a fresh-water sea, of which there is no mention of anyone having seen the bounds," thereby describing the route that French and English fur traders used to reach the Great Lakes, via the Mattawa River, Lake Nipissing, and the French River, for almost two and a half centuries, beginning in the early 1600s. Cartier learned also that the Richelieu River, which enters the St. Law-rence from the south at Lac Saint-Pierre, came from a land to the southwest where snow never fell and an abundance of fruit grew. Cartier presumed this land to be Florida, then the general name for Spain's claims in North America. (The Richelieu in fact springs from Lake Champlain, on the present-day border between the states of New York and Vermont.)

Still curious about the shadowy "kingdom of Saguenay," Cartier pressed the Iroquois for details. Donnaconna claimed that he had himself visited Saguenay and en-thusiastically informed the captain that there were "im-mense quantities of gold, rubies and other rich things [there], and that the men there are as white as in France and go clothed in woolens." Though Cartier would not have the opportunity to search any further for Saguenay—

he had determined to return to France as soon as the spring breakup allowed—he thought that Francis I ought to hear about this elusive New World land. Accordingly, on May 3, 1536, as the French raised a 35-foot cross to symbolize their laying claim to Canada, Donnaconna, Taignoagny, Domagaya, and four others were seized and hustled aboard the French vessels, leaving their people "howling and crying like wolves all night long, calling out incessantly. . . in the hope of being able to speak to [Donnaconna]." The next morning, when they gathered on the shore in preparation for an attack, Cartier compelled the chief to address his people, and Donnaconna quelled their fears by assuring them—as he had been assured by his captors—that he would be returned from France within a year. On May 6, 1536, leaving behind him the bodies of 25 of his countrymen and the hulk of *La Petite Hermine*, Cartier set sail.

On May 3, 1536, the feast day of the Holy Cross, Cartier used the raising of a huge cross on shore near his ships' anchorage as a ruse to carry out the kidnapping of Donnaconna and several other Indians. Of the 10 Indians that Cartier brought with him back to France, not one was ever returned to his homeland.

To Enter Deeper into These Lands

Cartier's return to Saint-Malo on July 16, 1536, did not come at a propitious moment, for France was just about to go to war with Spain, which meant that any plans to follow up on his latest expedition had to be postponed. It was not until the following year that Cartier (with Donnaconna) met with the king regarding his most recent travels and described the great river he had discovered, which was some 800 leagues (at least 2,000 miles) long, he said, and might well lead to Asia; the old Iroquois chief added fantastical details.

Though Francis I was now determined to obtain his own overseas empire—Spain was using New World gold to finance its wars with France, and Portugal was growing rich dealing in slaves and spices from the East—he was made leery of the expense by Cartier's somewhat grandiose plans for establishing a colony along the St. Lawrence and did not officially authorize a new expedition for several years. In the meantime, Cartier occupied himself plundering Spanish and Portuguese ships in *La Grande Hermine*— which the king had granted to him as a reward for his service—and possibly aiding rebellions against the king of England in Ireland. Finally, on October 17, 1540, by which time Donnaconna and all but 1 of the 10 Indians who had been brought back to France had died, Cartier received his new commission. He was charged this time with journeying to the lands of "Canada and Ochelaga and as far

King Francis I of France, by François Clouet, official court painter. Though an indifferent patron of exploration, Francis was responsible for introducing the ideas of the Italian Renaissance in France. He suffered, wrote Parkman, from an attention divided between "the smiles of his mistresses and the assaults of his enemies," Charles V of Spain being the foremost of the latter.

as the land of Saguenay, if he can reach it . . . to enter deeper into these lands, to converse with the peoples found there and to live among them, if need be," but not specifically to found a colony.

In January of the new year 1541, Francis appointed a new leader of the expedition: Jean-François de La Rocque, sieur de Roberval, a descendant of high-ranking nobility, a military officer, and a member of the king's immediate entourage. Roberval was to establish "towns and forts, temples and churches," institute laws so that the Indians might live "with reason and order in the fear and love of God," and exercise such absolute power over both the expedition and the proposed settlement that it was reported to Charles V of Spain that he had been appointed king of Canada. Cartier himself was now to come under Roberval's command. Though the Saint-Malo mariner had been the one who brought Canada to Francis's attention, he was a commoner, and though Roberval had never been to sea the establishment and government of a royal colony could be entrusted only to a noble.

Cartier's thoughts about this new arrangement are not known, but in his customary fashion he did a thorough job of preparing for the expedition. Entrusted with outfitting five ships, he bought enough food for two years and took on board various kinds of livestock—sheep, goats, cattle, swine, horses, and chickens. When the reports of Canada as an icebound land where scurvy was prevalent made it difficult for Roberval to recruit enough gentlemen and even "common folk" for the venture, even with the enticement of land and shares in a company that would divide the wealth of the colony, Francis I decided to empty the prisons. The only convicts ineligible for this New World parole were heretics, traitors, and counterfeiters; the crew for Cartier's five ships therefore included murderers and thieves among its number, as well as the first French-woman to visit the New World, Manon Lescault, the 18-year-old fiancée of one of the convicts.

Cartier's five ships—*La Grande Hermine*, *L'Emerillon*, *Saint-Brieux*, *Saint-Georges*, and a vessel whose name is not known—set sail from Saint-Malo on May 23, 1541. As Roberval's ships were not yet ready, the king ordered Cartier to start first; he arrived at Stadacona exactly three months later. (No details of the outward voyage are known, and in general less is known about Cartier's third voyage than about the first two.) The joyful reception he received there was not lessened even when he informed the village's inhabitants that Donnaconna had died, although he was not as forthcoming about the fate of the others. The other Indians, he told the Stadacona Iroquois, had all married, were living like "great lords" in France, and did not wish to return.

Though the Indians of Stadacona seemed to accept his explanation, Cartier sensed that his failure to return their friends and kin had jeopardized his relations with them, and he decided to make his headquarters farther upriver this time. After scouting ahead in a longboat, he decided on a spot past the mouth of the Chaudière River, known today as Cap Rouge, and brought all five of his ships upstream. He and his men found much to admire about this location. "On both sides of the river," the expedition narrative reads, "there are very good and fair grounds, full of as fair and mighty trees as any be in the world . . . [and] Vines, which we found laden with grapes as black as mulberries. . . . [I]t is as good a country to plow and manure as a man should find or desire." Better still, they discovered "a goodly mine of the best [i]ron in the world"; "leaves of fine gold as thick as a man's nail"; and "stones like diamonds, the most fair, polished and excellently cut that it is possible to see," which "[w]hen the sun shine upon them. . . glisten like sparkles of fire."

Cartier supervised the construction of a fort at the foot of a steep cliff, and a second fort above it on the cliff's summit, to protect the one below and provide a good view of the river. He had his men plow an acre and a half of land and

The reasons why Jean-François de La Rocque, sieur de Roberval, should have been granted such all-encompassing authority on Cartier's last voyage remain obscure. Though Roberval was a nobleman, he had never been to sea, and he had not done the Crown any signal services. Moreover, he was a Protestant, and one of the express purposes of the last expedition was to convert the Indians to Catholicism.

This illustration of Hochelaga appeared in the Italian version of Cartier's narratives that was published in 1556. Cartier described Hochelaga as "circular" and "completely enclosed by a wooden palisade in three tiers like a pyramid," consisting of "some fifty houses. . . each about fifty or more paces in length, and twelve or fifteen in width, built completely of wood and covered in and boarded up with large pieces of the bark and rind of trees."

plant it with cabbages, turnips, and other vegetables, which sprang up out of the ground in no time. The *Saint-Brieux* and the *Saint-Georges* were sent back to France, carrying aboard them samples of the "precious" metals and stones the explorers believed they had found. With the groundwork for the colony, which he called Charlesbourg Royal, thus laid, Cartier turned his attention to more exciting work: the discovery of the fabulous kingdom of Saguenay.

Leaving Charlesbourg Royal under the command of his brother-in-law, the vicomte de Beaupré, Cartier set out on September 7 with a small party in two boats. His destination was Hochelaga, where he hoped "to view and understand the fashion of the *Saults* [rapids] of water, which are to be passed to go to Saguenay." Armed with this knowledge, he would mount a full-fledged expedition to Saguenay the following spring. En route, he stopped at

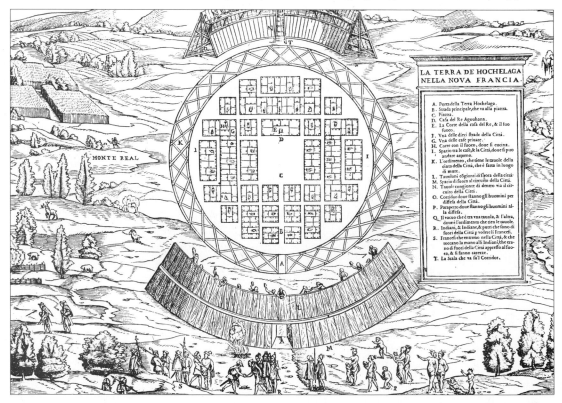

Achelacy, where the chief remembered him and greeted him with much affection. Cartier left two young French boys with the chief so that they might learn the Iroquois language, thereby beginning what became the traditional French method for training interpreters in New World languages.

At Montreal Island on September 11, Cartier's progress was stopped by "bad ground and great rocks, and so great a current, that we could not possibly pass any further," even though he had one of the boats "double-manned"—loaded with an extra crew to fight the rough water. On foot, Cartier and his men followed a well-traveled trail to an Indian village, four of whose inhabitants then guided them farther along the trail to another village, nearer the Lachine Rapids. The inhabitants of this last village indicated, by means of a map made out of sticks on the ground, that another great rapid stood between the explorers and Saguenay. Apparently, neither of these villages was Hochelaga, which receives no mention in the narrative of the last expedition. Whether it had been destroyed or abandoned in the intervening six years, or whether Cartier, for reasons unknown, decided not to return there, is unclear.

Since his sole purpose in coming upriver had been to "view . . . the fashion of the saults," Cartier now decided to turn back. A large group of Indians saw him off with effusive demonstrations of goodwill, although this friendliness may have been feigned. According to the author of the expedition narrative, "a man must not trust them for all their fair ceremonies and signs of joy, for if they had thought they had been too strong for us, then would they have done their best to have killed us, as we understood afterward."

On his way back to Charlesbourg Royal, Cartier stopped at Achelacy, where he had left the two French boys, but he found the village nearly empty and its chief gone. One of the chief's sons told Cartier that his father was visiting the

Indian village of Maisouna, but what had actually happened, apparently, was that the chief had gone to meet with Agona, Donnaconna's successor as chief at Stadacona, in order to plan an attack against the French. The expedition narrative provides no clues as to what might have caused relations between the French and Iroquois to deteriorate so drastically, but many of the would-be colonists at Charlesbourg Royal were career criminals, and it is not unreasonable to assume that some of them committed transgressions against the Indians, especially as, according to Jean Alfonce, a Frenchman with whom Donnaconna had spoken in France, the explorers had mistreated the Indians on their previous visit by stealing food and other goods, enforcing their will at sword point, and misbehaving with the Indian women. Moreover, there may have been lingering resentment on the part of the Iroquois regarding Cartier's broken promise to return Donnaconna and the other Indians safely to Stadacona. For any or all of these reasons, or perhaps simply out of foresight—this was, after all, the first time that their visitors had indicated that they were going to establish a permanent presence—the Indians of the St. Lawrence Valley now perceived the French as a threat.

In any event, upon his return to Charlesbourg Royal, Cartier found relations between the French and the Indians to be in a very bad state. The Indians, according to his narrative, "came not anymore about our Fort as they were accustomed . . . and . . . were in a wonderful doubt and fear of us." When several of Cartier's men informed him that "a wonderful number of the country people [were] assembled" at Stadacona, Cartier had the forts strengthened in anticipation of an attack.

Barricaded in their fortresses, the French suffered another hellish winter. Scurvy made its grim reappearance, though it was successfully treated with the annedda potion, and, Cartier told Roberval, "the Savages . . . went about daily to annoy him." Their raids claimed the life of several of the

It is uncertain upon what source Thevet relied for this engraving, which he entitled Tricks of War Among the Canadians, *for Cartier never accompanied the Indians on any of their raids. Nevertheless, he could attest to the cleverness of the St. Lawrence Iroquois as warriors, for they killed more than 35 of his men during the last winter he spent in Canada.*

colony's carpenters and perhaps as many as 35 of the colonists, and by the spring of 1542 it was clear to Cartier that the tiny colony could no longer defend itself.

In June, Cartier ordered the abandonment of Charlesbourg Royal and sailed with the settlers for France. At Newfoundland, in the middle of the month, Cartier met up at last with Roberval, who had not sailed for the New World until April 16, 1542. Despite Cartier's warnings about the danger of Indian attack there, the nobleman ordered the commoner to turn his ships around and return to Charlesbourg Royal, but in the middle of the night Cartier and his three ships "stole privily away," eager to present to King Francis I the 11 barrels of "gold," basket of "precious stones such as rubies and diamonds," and 7 barrels of "silver" his men had gathered. He arrived in Saint-Malo in October 1542, and though he was welcomed as a hero by the townspeople, the king's assayers soon disabused him of his notions regarding the worth of the "treasure" he had brought back with him: The "gold" was nothing more than iron pyrite, a glittery metal known popularly as fool's gold, the silver some other shimmering junk, and the "diamonds" quartz crystal, pretty but worth little. *Un diamant du Canada*

Cartier divided the days remaining to him after his last voyage to the New World between his farmhouse in the countryside (seen here) and his home in Saint-Malo, where his name appears often in church records as a guest at baptisms and weddings. Though his accomplishments were all but ignored for several centuries, he is remembered today as one of the master mariners of his age.

(a Canadian diamond) became a phrase used commonly in France to refer to any falsely alluring thing whose shiny surface misled the observer regarding its true value.

Meanwhile, Roberval had continued on through the Strait of Belle Isle and up the St. Lawrence. (En route, in anger over an illicit love affair, he marooned his young niece, her lover, and her nurse on a stony island off the Newfoundland coast. There, they managed to build a cabin, but that first winter the lover died. So, too, that following spring, did the child born to Marguerite de La Rocque as a result of her affair and, the next winter, her nurse. Improbably, the young woman managed to survive for more than two years, fighting off bears—she killed three, all of them as "white as an egg"—and tormented in her solitude by what she said were the voices of demons howling outside her cabin. These infernal spirits raged louder when she fired a gun, but they quieted when she read the New Testament aloud. At last, after 29 months, she was rescued by the crew of a French fishing vessel who saw the smoke from her cabin.) At the former site of Charlesbourg Royal, he built a new settlement, France-Roy, which consisted of a hillside fortress with lookout towers, a log palisade, soldiers' barracks, grain mills, a baking oven, a headquarters building, and sleeping quarters.

But Roberval had no more luck establishing a French foothold in the New World than did Cartier. Fifty of his colonists died of scurvy during the winter of 1542–43, and the rest almost perished from starvation: On most days, eight colonists had to collectively make do with two loaves of bread, a pound and a half of bacon, half a pound of beef, and some beans; on "fast days"—every Wednesday, Friday, and Saturday—those rations were reduced to a spoonful of beans and a few slivers of salted codfish or porpoise. Those who grumbled too much about conditions in the colony— Roberval brought with him mostly gentlemen recruits seduced by the promise of land and an easy fortune to be made in the New World—or otherwise misbehaved were whipped or thrown into irons, men and women alike. Many of the transgressors were hanged, and a number, including several women, were shot.

In the spring, Roberval took eight boats and 70 men upriver to look for Saguenay, but the mythical kingdom remained elusive. One of the boats was wrecked in the Lachine Rapids, and eight men drowned. Downstream below France-Roy and Stadacona, Jean Alfonce, Roberval's pilot, explored a short distance up the Saguenay River and concluded that it was an "arm of the sea" that "leads to the Pacific Ocean or even to the Sea of Cathay," but he went no farther. By that time, Roberval, like Cartier before him, had decided that Canada was too forbidding an environment to allow for permanent settlement, and he returned to his homeland, where he died in 1561, a victim of the religious and civil strife that dominated the middle decades of the 16th century in France. By that date, Cartier had himself been dead four years. Francis I had rewarded him with ownership of *L'Emerillon* as well as *La Grande Hermine*, and his years after his New World adventures were spent in well-fed comfort as one of Saint-Malo's first citizens, a frequent host at his home in town or farm in the countryside of nautical gatherings at which old salts like himself and England's Sebastian Cabot, a fellow searcher for the Northwest Passage, would hold forth endlessly with rollicking tales of their seafaring days.

Though Cartier's explorations left the cosmographers of the day with a much clearer picture of the geography of the northern regions of the New World, his and Roberval's dispiriting attempts to establish a colony along the St. Lawrence marked the end, for nearly six decades, of any action on the part of France's monarchs aimed at establishing an overseas empire in Canada, and the newfound lands were left once again to the fishermen of Brittany and Normandy.

Return to the St. Lawrence

While France's monarchy was preoccupied with the warfare between Catholics and Protestants that divided its populace during the middle decades of the 16th century, fishermen continued to visit Newfoundland, the Gulf of St. Lawrence, and the St. Lawrence River in huge numbers. In 1545, two French ships a day sailed for Newfoundland. Twenty years later, Pedro Menéndez, a Spanish mariner, complained that French fisherman "ruled despotically" over the waters of Newfoundland. In 1578, nearly 400 fishing vessels were counted in Canadian waters. One hundred and fifty of these were French; the remainder were Spanish, Portuguese, English, or Basque. In 1607, testimony was taken from an old French fisherman who said that he had visited the waters of Canada every year for the last forty-two.

These fishermen soon came to realize that the native inhabitants were eager to trade with them, especially if they could obtain metal goods and woven cloth and blankets. In exchange for these items, which were not of especially great value to the Europeans, they were willing to give furs, especially bear skins and beaver skins. Fur was a luxury in Europe, but to the Indians, surrounded by endless forest in which an unimaginable (to the Europeans) profusion of fur-bearing animals made their home, animal pelts were not an especially valued commodity. Thus, there were grounds for a commerce that both sides regarded as profitable. Exchanges were made at the many fishing sta-

This 1854 lithograph of Samuel de Champlain presents what has become a standard depiction of the explorer and founder of New France. Except for his own unrevealing drawings, no likenesses of Champlain from his own lifetime exist; Samuel Eliot Morison, one of his many biographers, believes that he was "a well-built man of medium stature, blond and bearded, a natural leader who inspired loyalty and commanded obedience."

tions the French established on Newfoundland and the mainland for the purpose of drying codfish before transporting it back to France. (Dried fish kept better than fish that was heavily salted, which was the earlier method of preservation.) In a short time, fishing vessels were returning to France with bear skins as well as dried cod, and most fishing captains engaged in a little trading on the side. By the end of the 16th century, as the beaver hat was becoming the most indispensable single item of fashionable gentlemen's wear in Europe, French mariners had established a number of fur-trading stations in Canada, most notably at Anticosti and Tadoussac, near the mouth of the Saguenay River, and former fishermen from Saint-Malo were setting out for the New World for the sole purpose of trading.

This commercial activity eventually caused renewed interest in Canada on the part of France's government. In 1598, a feckless Breton nobleman, Troilus de Mesgouez, marquis de La Roche, obtained from King Henri IV the title of lieutenant-general of Canada, Hochelaga, Newfoundland, Labrador, and all the countries adjacent, with

A Native American offers furs for trade in this somewhat fanciful engraving. In the final decades of the 16th century, merchant vessels from France, England, Spain, Portugal, and the Netherlands regularly visited the Grand Banks and Newfoundland to fish and trade for furs with the natives.

unlimited sovereign power within these domains. But this cumbersome title brought with it weighty responsibilities, to which La Roche proved unsuited: He was to found a colony that would serve as the beginnings of New France, as France's overseas empire in the New World would be known.

La Roche's colonists, according to Francis Parkman, were "a gang of thieves and desperadoes" culled from France's dungeons and jails. While he and the few gentlemen volunteers he had been able to recruit went scouting for a likely site on which to establish New France's capital, the convicts were left behind on uninhabited Sable Island, off the coast of Nova Scotia. There they waited five years for the return of La Roche, whose ship, tormented by storms, had long since returned to France, where he was promptly thrown into prison for his malfeasance.

An early-17th-century navigational chart of the Gulf of St. Lawrence and nearby areas. Sable Island, where the marquis de La Roche marooned 40 convicts-turned-colonists, is at bottom, just left of center. Fortunately for the castaways, Sable Island was inhabited by a herd of wild cattle, origin unknown, which provided them a source of food.

French admiration for the industry and engineering skills of the beaver, as manifested in the complex dens and dams it builds, is evident in this early-18th-century engraving of the flat-tailed rodents at work. Beaver skins, which were used to make gentlemen's hats and fashionable accessories, were the most valuable of the many different kinds of pelts that could be obtained in Canada.

In the meantime, upon La Roche's return and subsequent disgrace a navy captain, Pierre Chauvin de Tonnetuit, was given his old commission: an exclusive monopoly over trade "in the country of Canada, the coast of Acadia [Nova Scotia and New Brunswick] and others of New France." Directed to "live in the country and build a stronghold," Chauvin proposed to bring 500 men and establish a colony at Tadoussac. With four ships, the biggest fleet to sail for Canada under one command since Cartier and Roberval, he set out for Canada in the spring of 1600, but at Tadoussac he directed most of his efforts to trading rather than establishing a functioning colony. He built only one, inadequate dwelling—Samuel de Champlain would later refer to it contemptuously as "a country cottage"—and returned to France with the first frost, leaving 16 "colonists" behind to fend for themselves. Ill equipped to cope with the severity of a Canadian winter, some of the colonists died; the rest were forced to abandon their "habitation" and take refuge with the local Indians. Chauvin sent a ship in the spring of 1601 with reinforcements and supplies, but the colony was abandoned by the start of the next winter.

On Sable Island, meanwhile, the marooned convicts fashioned crude cabins out of driftwood and the wreck of a boat they found on the beach, fished, and hunted foxes and seal. The climate and harshness of their existence ultimately claimed some, and others were murdered. By 1603, when a rescue ship at last reached the island, only 11 of the original 40 were still alive. Back in France, the castaways were summoned to meet with King Henri IV. "They stood before him," wrote Parkman, "like river-gods of yore; for from head to foot they were clothed in shaggy skins, and beards of prodigious length hung from their swarthy faces." The survivors did have something to show for their ordeal, however: a small fortune in pelts. This reward for their endurance was sufficient to convince Henri and others that the goal of establishing a French colony was worth pursuing, though their suffering (as well as the experiences of Cartier, Roberval, and Chauvin) was ample demonstration that the founding of New France would require the energies of a truly remarkable individual.

Samuel de Champlain was born sometime around 1570 in Brouage, a little seaport in Saintonge, the French province just south of Brittany. Little is known of his childhood, other than that his father was one Antoine de Complain, a sea captain, and his mother was Dame Margueritte Le Roy. He was probably born a Protestant and only later coverted to Catholicism. Despite his use of the noble title *sieur* in later life, he was neither born nor raised to the nobility.

Champlain was apparently drawn to the sea as a young man, judging by his 1613 declaration that navigation was the art that "from my early age has won my love, and induced me to expose myself almost all my life to the impetuous waves of the ocean." Nothing is known about his education, but the many maps and pictures that he drew in later life indicate that he received some kind of artistic training, and he was an entertaining and observant writer.

The first historical record of Champlain indicates that in the early 1590s he served in the army of Brittany as a quartermaster. In 1632, he stated that he had in fact fought against the Catholic League in the army of Henri IV until 1598, with the rank of sergeant. At war's end, he sailed to Spain with his uncle, Guillaume Hellaine, whose ship the *Saint-Julian* had been commissioned to return the defeated Spanish troops to their homeland.

In January 1599, after four months in various Spanish ports, the *Saint-Julian* was chartered for a trading expedition to the West Indies and Central America. Champlain thus spent the next 22 months sailing the Caribbean and the south Atlantic, in the process visiting most of the important colonies of New Spain, including New Granada (present-day Colombia, Venezuela, Ecuador, and Panama), Mexico, Cuba, and Puerto Rico. In the course of this voyage, he attained a reputation as a masterful navigator, and when he returned to France in 1601 he was given a pension and an honorary title at the court of Henri IV. He spent at least a portion of the next two years writing an account of his travels, a 115-page manuscript, illustrated with 62 of his own drawings, lengthily entitled, in the fashion of the day, *Brief Discourse of the most remarkable things which Samuel Champlain of Brouage has observed in the West Indies during the voyages he made thither in the year 1599 and the year 1601, as follows.*

In 1603, at the king's behest, Aymar de Chaste, who on Chauvin's death had been awarded the royal monopoly on the Canada trade, outfitted a fresh expedition of colonization. As the commander of his fleet, de Chaste selected François Gravé Du Pont, a 50-year-old veteran of several fishing voyages to the St. Lawrence. At the king's urging, Gravé Du Pont asked Champlain to accompany him and prepare a report on the endeavor for Henri.

With his three ships, Gravé Du Pont left Honfleur, in Normandy, on March 15, 1603, and arrived at Tadoussac near the end of May. The Montagnais and Algonquin Indians of the region proved eager to trade, and Champlain described their appearance and customs at great length in his published account of the expedition, *The Savages, or, A Voyage by Samuel Champlain of Brouage.* Guided by some Montagnais, on June 11 he traveled, using a pinnace and longboat, some 35 or 40 miles up the Saguenay, farther than any European before him. He learned from his Indian guides that farther upriver were 18 falls and rapids, beyond which lay a great lake (Lac Saint-Jean) fed by several other rivers. If one then traveled up the principal of these rivers flowing from the north (the Ashuapmuchuan), one passed through a series of lakes, then finally reached a vast "salt-water sea."

Instead of assuming that this saltwater sea was the Pacific, as the other explorers of Canada before him had been all too eager to do when presented with information about large bodies of water to the west, Champlain, in his account of the expedition, asserted it must be "some gulf of this our

Canadians kill buffalo in this 1575 Thevet woodcut. According to many of the sailors and fishermen he spoke with—Thevet made it a practice to interview all those who returned from New World voyages—buffalo were then numerous in the St. Lawrence region and could even be found on the island of Anticosti.

These drawings of some of the ships in which Champlain sailed to the New World are taken from his famous map of 1612. Champlain's seamanship is often overshadowed by his New World explorations, but he was a masterful sailor who crossed the dangerous North Atlantic 23 times without mishap and penned a classic work on ship management, Treatise on Seamanship and the Duty of a Good Seaman.

sea [the Atlantic], which overflows in the north into the midst of the continent." Intuitively, Champlain thus divined the existence of Hudson Bay, seven years before its discovery by the English, and he gleaned from the Indians a complete picture of the Saguenay basin and its waterways. (His uncanny geographical instinct was one of the most admirable aspects of Champlain's remarkable character. In his manuscript on his West Indies voyage, for example, he outlined the many benefits that would be gained if a way could be found to cut a canal across Panama "so that the whole of America would be in two islands" and the Atlantic and the Pacific oceans connected.)

After the fur trading had been concluded, Gravé Du Pont, with Champlain, headed up the St. Lawrence, as far as the Lachine Rapids (which Champlain called Sault Saint-Louis). Though the expedition added nothing to the existing knowledge of the river itself, other than a few freshly coined place names, Champlain did provide a more detailed and clearer description of the river than had Cartier, and he proved a master at eliciting useful geographical information—as opposed to tall tales about the kingdom of Saguenay, for example—from the Indians. He obtained a reliable description of the Richelieu and Ottawa rivers, soon to be crucial waterways in the fur trade, and was able to form a reasonably accurate conception of the Great Lakes network. He was also much taken with what he referred to in his account as Quebec, the former site of Stadacona, which like Hochelaga had been abandoned by its inhabitants. To Champlain, Quebec immediately suggested itself as a likely site for the capital of a new colony, although his attention was soon turned elsewhere. (Quebec was Champlain's transcription of an Indian word that meant the place where the river narrows.)

Champlain and Gravé Du Pont departed Tadoussac on July 11 for the Gaspé Peninsula, where they remained until the 19th. Again, by speaking with the Indians, Champlain was able to gather an enormous amount of geographical information, as well as reports about the alleged mineral wealth of Acadia. These reports seemed to be confirmed by the experience of the Saint-Malo mariner Sarcel de Prévert, whom Gravé Du Pont and Champlain met up with on August 18 en route to the Grand Banks of New-foundland. Prévert claimed to have visited several rich copper mines near what is now called the Bay of Fundy, although he was in truth repeating hearsay rather than recounting his actual experience.

Nonetheless, Acadia, rather than the St. Lawrence Val-ley, now seemed to Champlain to hold the greatest prospect for colonization, by virtue of the presence of the alleged mines, the purported beauty and fertility of the countryside, its warmer climate, and the alleged greater peacefulness of its Indians. His reasoning, upon his return to France in September 1603, helped convince Pierre de Gua, sieur de Monts, the recently deceased de Chaste's successor as the holder of the royal fur-trading monopoly, to concentrate his colonization efforts on Acadia.

Commissioned once again by Henri IV to act as expedi-tion chronicler, Champlain set out with de Monts for Acadia in September 1604. (His account of the Gravé Du Pont expedition, his first published book, first appeared in Paris in late 1603.) After some initial reconnoitering of prospective sites in the Bay of Fundy, de Monts and Champlain, whose mastery of navigation had made him invaluable to the expedition commander, chose an island (known today as Dochet Island) near the mouth of the St. Croix River as the best spot to establish a colony. (The St. Croix constitutes the southernmost portion of the pre-sent-day border between New Brunswick and the state of Maine.)

The settlement at Sainte-Croixe was constructed around an elm-shaded central plaza and consisted of a house for de Monts, a lengthy covered gallery, common barracks for the 120 colonists, a couple of blocks of houses for the several officers, a small rectory and chapel, a smithy, an outdoor oven for baking bread, and a kitchen overhanging the river. Although the site quickly proved to have been poorly chosen—the sandy soil would not grow vegetables, and the only source of fresh water was on the mainland—the settlers nonetheless harbored optimism for the success of their endeavor; that is, until winter set in.

"It is impossible to know this country without having wintered there," Champlain wrote, "for on arriving in autumn everything is very pleasant owing to the woods, the fair landscape, and the good fishing for cod and other species which we found. But winter in this country lasts for six months." And as the winds howled and the snow fell and the ice grew ever thicker between the island and the mainland, the colonists inexorably sickened and died, most of them from scurvy, which "raged with a fearful malignity," according to Parkman. Nearly half were dead by springtime.

By the time the next winter rolled in, the colony had been relocated, to a site the settlers called Port Royal (present-day Annapolis Royal) across the Bay of Fundy on the west coast of Nova Scotia. A settlement similar to Sainte-Croixe was built there, with the addition of a few homier touches, foremost among them Champlain's private garden, where he fashioned a saltwater pond for cod and perch. "We often went there," he wrote, "to pass the time; and it seemed to please the little birds of the neighborhood; for they assembled there in great numbers and made such a pleasant warbling and twittering, of which I have never heard the like." But the pleasantness of the habitation was no match for the ferocity of winter, and once again the colonists suffered terribly. Approximately one-quarter of them died of scurvy or other illnesses. The following winter claimed more. Even so, some of the survivors remained, and the colony at Port Royal hung on until 1613, when it was overrun and destroyed by English colonists from Virginia led by Sir Samuel Argall. (continued on page 73)

Whence They Came

King Francis I of France, with his court.

In the 16th century, France, of all the nations of Europe, would have seemed the most likely to establish itself as the dominant power in North America. Spain was more interested in the southerly regions of the Americas, from which it was extracting an unimaginable fortune in gold and silver, and Portugal had insufficient manpower even to maintain control over its trading colonies in the spice-producing lands of the fabled Indies. Italy and Germany were too divided politically and lacked sufficient economic incentive; Italy's city-states prospered from trade in the Mediterranean, and Germany's mercantile mariners enjoyed a virtual monopoly on the Baltic Sea trade with Scandinavia. The Netherlands was still struggling to attain its independence. Indeed, of Europe's seafaring nations only England and France had good reason to take an interest in North America, and of those two France might have been expected to emerge triumphant there: Its population was six times that of England, it possessed as much coastline, it was much wealthier, its mariners were more accomplished and were the first to regularly visit Canadian shores, and it possessed, under Francis I and later Henri IV, governments that took at least a cursory interest in New World exploration. Yet despite the promising beginnings made for France by Cartier and Champlain along the gulf and river of St. Lawrence, it was England that ultimately came to control all of eastern North America, in large part because France was never able to persuade sufficient numbers of its citizens to settle permanently in the wild regions visited by its brave explorers.

A more illustrative portrait of Francis, as done by his court painter, Jean Clouet. An exceptionally charming individual, Francis was generally well liked by his subjects, although he ruled with a heavy hand. His wars on the Continent left him unable to devote a great deal of attention or money to New World exploration and eventually left France bankrupt.

An early Italian Renaissance map of France. The premier seafaring areas of France were Brittany (the region jutting westernmost, designated Balle Bretaigne, Les Landes de Bretaigne, and Les haute Bretaigne on this map), Normandy (just east of Brittany, labeled Normandie), and Saintonge (Sainton, on the west coast, south of Brittany). Cartier was from Brittany, Champlain from Saintonge.

Jacques Cartier of Saint-Malo
was the individual Francis chose
to explore the northern extremities
of the coastline that Giovanni da
Verrazano had reconnoitered as far
south as the present-day Carolinas.
By the time of his selection by the
king, Cartier had attained the rank
of master pilot, an achievement
that in medieval France required as
much time and training as earning
a doctorate from a university.

This 1546 map, usually attributed to Nicholas Vallard, depicts the arrival of the colonists brought by Cartier and the sieur de Roberval to Canada in 1541 and 1542. Note the presence of women among the French party, the fur-clad Native Americans at the far left and the far right, and the bears and deer in the forest.

This map of North America was one of 56 maps drawn by the Norman sea captain and explorer Guillaume Le Testu, whose atlas, Universal Cosmography, was published in 1556. Le Testu was accompanied on several of his voyages to the New World by André Thevet, who was also deeply interested in the explorations of Cartier.

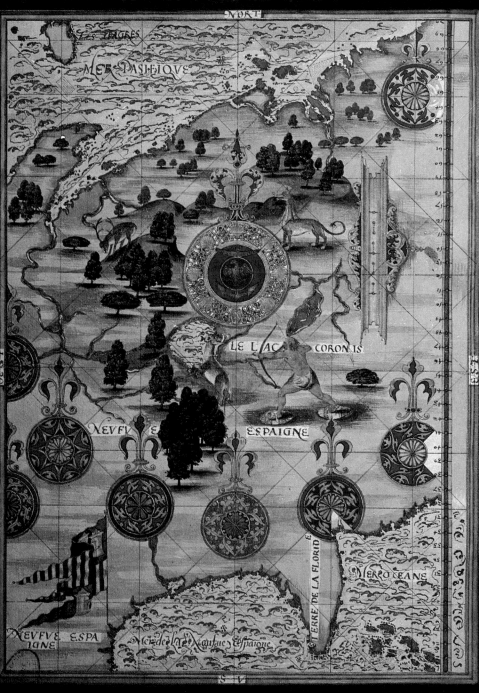

King Henri IV backed many of Champlain's voyages, but like his predecessors on the throne of France he was too preoccupied by troubles at home and elsewhere on the Continent to make overseas exploration a priority.

A 1700 map of New France, with a cutaway view of the city of Quebec, which Champlain had founded. France claimed most of the regions shown on this map, but in most areas its control was nominal at best, and it would be forced to relinquish all its New World claims, with the exception of some islands in the Caribbean, to England in 1763.

(continued from page 64)

Champlain shivered through these winters like the rest of the colonists, but he spent his summers systematically exploring by pinnace the Atlantic coastline as far south as Cape Cod, Massachusetts. The maps and harbor charts he prepared as a result of these reconnaissances were the most accurate and useful of any made of the region during the 17th century.

De Monts and Champlain returned to France in late September 1607. Champlain had been convinced by his Acadia experience that the St. Lawrence Valley was after all the best location for a French colony, and he now argued the point to de Monts: The Acadian winters had not been noticeably less harsh than what he expected would be the case along the St. Lawrence, and the river was a better fur-trading area and more easily defended from potentially covetous European enemies.

Though he wished to exploit his monopoly, which was due to expire in 1609, de Monts was not eager to return to Canada, so he appointed Champlain to command his next expedition. On April 13, 1608, three ships under Champlain's command set sail for Canada. Champlain's party, in

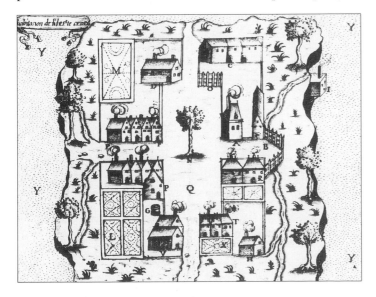

Champlain's drawing of the French colony of Sainte-Croixe, where the settlers endured a hellish winter. Champlain was never able to find the annedda trees that had served Cartier so well in fighting off the ravages of scurvy.

Near the site of the present-day town of Chatham, Massachusetts, on Cape Cod, which Champlain visited several times in the summer months of 1605 and 1606, five of his men were ambushed and killed by Nauset Indians after the French erected a huge cross. The Indians' disrespect was almost as galling to Champlain as their murderous behavior: As the French were leaving, the Indians tore down the cross, exhumed one of the corpses, and "turning their backs to the [ship], they did cast sand with their two hands betwixt their buttocks in derision, howling like wolves."

Le Don de Dieu, arrived at Tadoussac on June 3, and there met with an unpleasant surprise: a group of Basques, led by a man named Darache, had already entrenched themselves in the area and were actively engaged in the fur trade. When Gravé Du Pont, who by this point had become Champlain's great friend and would join him in most of his ventures, ordered them to leave the area, the Basques responded by opening fire. Gravé Du Pont was wounded and relieved of his arms, but a truce was soon arranged, and it was agreed that the dispute would be settled back in France.

On June 30, Champlain set out in a small bark up the St. Lawrence to the region that he knew as Quebec. At the foot of the great rock, where the river narrowed and a natural landing place presented itself, Champlain established, on July 3, 1608, the first permanent European settlement in what is now Canada. He had several build-

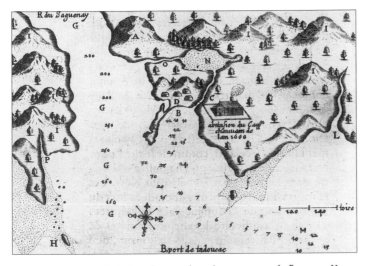

Champlain's chart of Tadoussac, a trading post at the mouth of the Saguenay River where Etchemins, Montagnais, and Algonquins brought furs to barter with the French.

ings constructed, joined together by a second-floor gallery and a continuous outside wall, around which were built a moat with drawbridge and a wooden palisade. Though he was now secure from outside attack, the ramparts of his stockade could not protect Champlain from betrayal from within. At the instigation of a locksmith named Jean Duval, Champlain was told by a conscience-stricken plotter, a group of conspirators had hatched a conspiracy to murder Champlain and deliver his fort into the hands of the Basques. Champlain arrested the unrepentant plotters and executed Duval, whose disembodied head, impaled on a pike, remained in plain view "from the highest roof of the buildings, food for birds and a lesson to sedition," according to Parkman. His accomplices were sent back to France as prisoners with Gravé Du Pont on September 18.

Of the approximately 28 colonists who stayed behind with Champlain, only 8 survived scurvy to witness the spring of 1609. The Montagnais Indians of the area also suffered greatly, for that winter was light in game as well as snow, and many of them starved. Champlain described them as looking "like skeletons," and he fed them with the colony's supplies, hopeful that his charity would dispose them to look with kindness upon the French colony and make them eager to engage in the fur trade. In May 1609, Gravé Du Pont returned from France with additional supplies and colonists.

Following the return of his friend, Champlain decided to conduct a journey of exploration into the country to the south, which was dominated by the Five Nations of the Iroquois—the Mohawks, the Onondagas, the Senecas, the Cayugas, and the Oneidas. As he was preparing to leave, there appeared at Quebec a party of Algonquins, accompanied by several Indians of a sort never previously encountered by the French. The colonists dubbed the strangers *Huron*, on account of their hairstyle, which resembled the bristly ridge of a boar's head. (*Hure* means "boar's head" in French.) The Hurons, whose traditional homeland was between the Georgian Bay and Lake Simcoe, had long dominated trade on the Great Lakes, but they had grown accustomed to obtaining French trade goods from the tribes to the east and were now eager to enter into a direct alliance with the French, whom they called *agnonha* (the iron people).

Champlain traveled some distance upriver with his visitors—"the country becomes more and more beautiful as you advance," he noted in the first volume of his *Voyages*, which appeared in 1613—to a conference with chiefs of the Hurons, Algonquins, and Montagnais. In the hope of securing a trade alliance with these peoples, Champlain agreed to join them in a campaign against the Iroquois, whose constant raids made them the scourge of the northern tribes. On June 28, with 20 Frenchmen in two small shallops and several thousand Indians in birchbark canoes, Champlain set out. At the mouth of the Richelieu River, a great ceremonial feast was held. The revelry lasted for several days; when it was concluded, almost all the Indian warriors decided to go home "with their wives and the wares they had bartered," Champlain wrote.

His war party now reduced to just 60 Indians and 20 Frenchmen, Champlain traveled up the Richelieu to the falls at Chambly, where he and two other Frenchmen abandoned their boats in favor of canoes. (The rest of the French were sent back to Quebec.) On July 14, Champlain's party arrived at the source of the Richelieu, a huge lake—430 miles wide by 125 miles long—that lies on the present-day border between the states of New York and Vermont. He named it after himself; on July 29, at its southern end, near the future site of Fort Ticonderoga, his party encountered about 200 Mohawk warriors, "strong, robust men [who] came slowly to meet us with a gravity and calm which I admired." The ensuing battle was decided in favor of the French party by virtue of the firepower and shock value of their arquebuses (a cumbersome, primitive rifle fired with a matchlock). Champlain's party suffered no casualties; about 50 Iroquois were killed, and several dozen were captured. The battle had the desired effect for Champlain and the French of securing the friendship of the Hurons and Algonquins; it was also the first incident in a long history of enmity between the French and the Five Nations of the Iroquois.

Champlain's drawing of the habitation at Quebec, which was surrounded by a moat, gallery, and promenade. The section labeled H was his own quarters.

Champlain's drawing of the fight between his Indian allies and the Iroquois at Lake Champlain, where the firepower of the arquebus decided the day. His depiction of the Indians as naked is a bow to artistic convention at the expense of historical accuracy: European readers of New World exploration narratives had come to expect to hear tales of "naked savages."

Following his skirmish with the Iroquois, Champlain returned to Quebec and then sailed for France with Gravé Du Pont. He arrived in Honfleur on October 13, 1609, then proceeded to Fontainebleau to make his report to de Monts and Henri IV. Champlain presented the king with a Mohawk scalp, a belt of porcupine quills, the skull of a garfish, and two live scarlet tanagers, but though Henri expressed "pleasure and satisfaction" with the explorer's efforts, he refused to extend de Monts's monopoly. Champlain and de Monts decided to carry on with the colonization effort anyway, backed financially by some merchants from the city of Rouen.

Champlain returned to Quebec in early May 1610. He was pleased to discover that the winter of his absence had been unusually mild and that a steady supply of fresh game had kept the colony free from scurvy. "Which goes to

show," he wrote, "that you can't expect to have everything nice your first year, but that by doing without salt provisions and having fresh meat, one's health is as good there as in France." Though he pleaded with the Hurons and Algonquins to guide him up the St. Maurice River and other waterways to Hudson Bay, they begged instead for him to lead an attack against an Iroquois war party that, seeking revenge for the Lake Champlain rout, was encamped on the Richelieu about four miles from its mouth, and he complied with their entreaties. Despite being wounded by an arrow that "split the tip of my ear and pierced my neck," Champlain led his forces to victory. It was to be his last triumph over the Iroquois.

Following this battle, as a further bond of their friendship, Champlain entrusted young Étienne Brûlé, a boy who had been one of the founders of Quebec, to his Indian friends so that he could "learn what was the nature of their country, see the great lake, observe the rivers, what manner of people inhabit them; withal to discover what mines and most rare things may be found among these places and peoples." In return, Champlain accepted custody of Savignon, a Huron who wanted to visit France. Brûlé soon became the first European to travel up the Ottawa River, to visit Algonquin country, and to see the Great Lakes.

Upon his return to Quebec, Champlain was faced with a disturbing situation. As a result of a surfeit of French fur traders along the St. Lawrence, 1610 had been a disastrous year for the fur trade for all involved, and without adequate revenues de Monts's company could do little to support Quebec. To make matters worse, King Henri IV had been assassinated, and with him died any hope of royal protection from unauthorized competitors in the fur trade for Champlain and de Monts. Champlain decided to return to France in order to attempt to clarify the situation. Leaving 16 men behind at Quebec, he sailed on August 8, 1610, and arrived at Honfleur almost seven weeks later.

One of the means by which the determined Champlain
contrived to save Quebec was matrimony. On December
30, 1610, he married Hélène Boullé, the 12-year-old
daughter of the secretary of the king's chamber. Although
the contract specified that the marriage would not be
consummated for two years in consideration of the girl's
tender age, the 40-year-old Champlain received three-
quarters of the considerable dowry up front. He used a
significant portion of it to obtain living quarters and ser-
vants for his wife in Paris, then immediately set to outfitting his next expedition. He sailed for Quebec on March
1, 1611.

Shortly after his arrival in late May, he departed Quebec
and traveled upriver to the Lachine Rapids, where he had
arranged previously to meet a party of Algonquin fur
traders. Though the Indians did not show up, Champlain's
trip was not wasted, as he surveyed the area with the idea
of establishing a second colony nearby. On the island of
Montreal, on a point of land later to be known as Ponte
Callières, he built a wall some 10 yards long, 4 feet wide,
and 3 or 4 feet high, so he could see how the clay he used
would hold up to the ravages of winter. Though Montreal
would not be established as a permanent French settlement
until 1642, it soon became the site of the largest annual
gathering of French and Indian fur traders.

The Hurons and Algonquins, some 200 of them, in the
company of Étienne Brûlé, who was dressed "as a savage"
and had "most excellently learned. . . [their] tongue,"
appeared at last on June 13. During the parley, feast, and
exchange of goods that then ensued, Champlain greatly
impressed his Indian allies by shooting the Lachine Rapids
in a canoe. In so doing he at last broke through the barrier
that since Cartier's time had halted further European
progress up the St. Lawrence; before Champlain, Brûlé was
the only white man to have passed beyond the great rapids.

For some years, Champlain had been urging the Indians
to guide him on a northward voyage of exploration. Recog-

nizing that the less the French knew about the geography of the interior, the stronger their own position in the fur trade would be, and hoping to confine the newcomers to the St. Lawrence Valley, the Indians had always managed to put Champlain off with some kind of excuse, but now, perhaps seeing it as a way to strengthen their friendship with the French, the Indians themselves proposed such an expedition. (The Indians grew savvy about the fur trade in a hurry: They were already demanding a vastly higher quality of trade goods in exchange for the beaver, moose, wolf, fox, bear, otter, marten, fisher, and wolverine skins they brought the French.) Pressed by affairs in France that required his immediate attention—he sailed for home in August—Champlain sent in his stead a young man named Nicolas de Vignau, to whom he gave "a very precise memorandum of those things he should observe while among them."

The French, Huron, and Algonquin victory over the Iroquois encamped at the mouth of the Richelieu River in the summer of 1610 was to be the last time that Champlain would defeat the Iroquois in battle.

LOVIS XIII. ROY DE FRANCE
ET DE NAVARRE.

L. Gaultier inedit

Champlain Goes West

On arriving in France, Champlain hastened to Saintonge to consult with de Monts. Since their last meeting, de Monts had bought out his Rouen partners and enlisted the financial support of a group of merchants based in La Rochelle. In exchange for their investment, de Monts had ceded to these merchants the Quebec habitation with all fur trading rights, but because they had been unable to secure a monopoly, de Monts's new partners, Champlain learned, no longer wished to support the colony. And it was proving difficult for de Monts to drum up interest elsewhere, for excitement over the prospects of Brazil was attracting whatever French enthusiasm remained for overseas colonization. What de Monts proposed as a solution was enlisting as nominal head of the enterprise some person of high rank, whose prestige would help win support.

Desperate to save Quebec, Champlain turned for help to the new king, Louis XIII, who on October 8, 1612, named Charles de Bourbon, comte de Soissons, as his lieutenant general in New France. When de Soissons died shortly afterward, the king transferred the appointment to Henri de Bourbon, prince de Condé, who on November 22, 1612, chose Champlain as his own lieutenant. The appointment marked a rise in position and prestige for Champlain. Since 1608 he had been only the lieutenant of de Monts, a man of relatively little influence; now he was the deputy of the Prince de Condé, viceroy of New France. His commission, moreover, granted him the authority of a governor in New France, though he was not officially named as such.

Louis XIII was just nine years old when he succeeded the murdered Henri IV on the throne of France in 1610. Most of the Crown's business was actually conducted by his mother, Marie de Medici, and then by Cardinal Richelieu, the Eminence Rouge.

On May 14, 1610, François Ravaillac, a penniless former schoolteacher tormented by religious hallucinations, stabbed Henri IV to death as the king rode through the streets of Paris in the royal carriage. The assassination was the 20th attempt made on Henri's life during his tumultuous reign.

Under Condé, a new company was quickly formed and granted a monopoly on the fur trade by the king. The many rival traders who had been draining profits from de Monts's company and antagonizing the Indians through their unscrupulous practices would now be substantially restrained.

Though Champlain had many other affairs to occupy him in France besides the company's business—the publication of the first volume of his *Voyages*, which included many of his superb charts and maps, and the flight of his child-bride from their home being just two—he was most eager to sail for Canada. Nicolas de Vignau had returned to Paris in the summer of 1612, swearing that he had paddled up the Ottawa River from the Lachine Rapids and in just 17 days had reached the "Northern Sea" (Hudson Bay). He claimed to have seen, on the shores of the Northern Sea, the wreck of an English ship, whose crew of 80 had made it to shore but had subsequently been murdered by Indians, with the exception of a young boy whom the Indians had kept to present to Champlain. Champlain speculated that this wreck might be from Henry Hudson's voyage to the bay in 1610. "This intelligence," Champlain later wrote, "greatly pleased me, for I thought that I had almost found that for which I had for a long time been searching"; it seemed likely to Champlain and others that the so-called Northern Sea might contain the answer to the riddle of the Northwest Passage.

On learning of Vignau's assertions, French authorities, regarding the news of a British presence to the north as a threat to New France, asked Champlain to visit the bay in person. Champlain decided to retrace the route described by Vignau. He sailed for Canada on March 6, 1613, and arrived at Tadoussac on March 29. After announcing his new commission, he stopped briefly at Quebec, then went up to the Lachine Rapids, where he had arranged to meet with Indian fur traders. As in 1611, the Indians, angered by the tactics of the illegal fur traders, showed up only in small numbers. The small turnout affected Champlain's plans for his northern expedition as well as his profits. He had hoped to be taken up the Ottawa River by a convoy of Huron traders returning to their home villages, but he was able to obtain the services of only one Indian, who acted as a guide. As a result, Champlain was forced to transport himself and his party in their own canoes; he thus became the first of the legion of fur traders whose canoe voyages made them Canada's foremost explorers and would eventually carry them all the way to the Pacific.

Champlain began his first western exploration on May 27, 1613. With him, in two canoes, traveled the Indian guide and four Frenchmen, among them Vignau. By the 29th, they had passed the Lachine Rapids, "partly by

Canoes were the vessels that conquered Canada; the fur traders who followed Champlain to Canada would use the lightweight birch-bark vessels fashioned by the Ottawas, Hurons, and other tribes to travel the network of Canada's rivers from Lachine all the way to the Pacific. Bécard de Granville, a later French explorer of Canada, made these drawings of an Ottawa canoe (top) and a French modified version in the late 17th century.

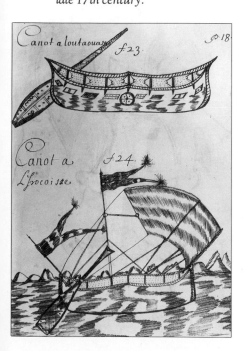

land, partly by water, it being necessary," according to Champlain, "for us to carry our canoes, clothes, victuals, and arms on our shoulders, no small matter for persons not accustomed to it." On the Ottawa, they soon reached a series of falls now known as the Long Sault, where they had to make a portage through thick woods without trails; at other points they were forced to get into the water and tow their canoes with ropes. On June 1, they encountered a particularly rough stretch where the current was "so great that it makes a frightful noise, and produces, as it descends from stage to stage, so white a foam everywhere that the water cannot be seen at all." As Champlain was towing his canoe, it got caught in a whirlpool. "If I had not had the good fortune to fall between two rocks," he wrote, "the canoe would have dragged me in, inasmuch as I was unable to undo quickly enough the rope which was wound around my hand, and which hurt me severely and came close to cutting it off." His companions had several similar escapades.

The next day, Champlain's group encountered a party of Algonquins paddling downstream in 15 canoes. The Indians had been informed of Champlain's coming, but they were astonished to see him traveling with such a small party and only one native guide. They warned him that what lay ahead upriver was much more difficult than anything he had yet seen. As it was becoming increasingly obvious that Vignau did not really know where he was going, and as his Indian guide was not very familiar with the country they were about to enter, Champlain asked the Algonquins to lend him another guide. This they gladly did; at the same time it was agreed that the least essential member of the French party would remain with the Indians and go downriver with them.

Champlain's new guide also took charge of one of the canoes, leaving both boats in the hands of expert native steersmen for the many dangerous rapids that still lay ahead. On June 4, where the Gatineau River enters from the north and the Rideau River from the south, the explorers passed the future site of the city of Ottawa; a little farther upstream they admired the magnificent falls now known as Chaudière. Champlain observed that the water at Chaudière fell in one place "with such force upon a rock that it has hollowed out in course of time a large and deep basin, in which the water has a circular motion and forms large eddies in the middle. . . . This cataract produces such a noise in this basin that it is heard for more than two leagues." The Indians, according to Champlain, performed propitiatory rites when passing this spot; they collected a dish of tobacco, around which they danced and sang, then threw the tobacco into the whirlpool as an offering.

Two long portages were required for Champlain and his men to pass Chaudière Falls. They then entered Lac des Chats, where they spent the night of June 5 and erected a cross. On the following day, at the northern end of the lake, which proved impassable, Champlain and his men, on the advice of their guide, portaged from a point now called Goulds Wharf (near Portage du Fort) to the slender chain of lakes and streams lying between the present Coldingham and Catherine lakes. The portage took an entire day and was extremely tiring. "We had much difficulty in going this distance overland," Champlain wrote. "I, for my part, was loaded only with three arquebuses, as many oars, my cloak, and some small articles. I cheered on our men, who were somewhat more heavily loaded, but more troubled by the mosquitoes than by their loads." The long haul left Champlain and his men "so wearied that it was impossible to go farther, not having eaten for twenty-four hours anything but a little broiled fish without seasoning, for we had left our provisions behind."

The explorers now left the Ottawa and paddled across Town Lake, Edmonds Lake, Olmsted Lake, and Green Lake, at whose northern end they began a long and exhausting portage during which their path was frequently blocked by fallen trees. In this region, in 1867, a farm boy found a bronze mariner's astrolabe dated 1603, which may have been dropped by Champlain. On reaching the southern end of Muskrat Lake, they were visited by a group of Indians, who were, according to Champlain, "astonished that we could have passed the falls and bad roads in order to reach them." Their chief, Nibachis, declared in an address to his people that the French "must have fallen from the clouds, for he knew not how we could have made the journey, and those who lived in the country had much trouble in traversing these bad ways." He then lent them two more canoes and the services of a couple of guides, who led Champlain's party across Muskrat Lake and over the so-called Stoqua Portage to a widening of the Ottawa River now called Lower Allumette Lake, which they reached on June 8.

The tiny band of explorers was now in the domain of the Algonquin chief Tessoüat, whom Champlain had met at Tadoussac in 1603 and in whose village Vignau had lived. Tessoüat, said Champlain, "was greatly amazed to see me, saying that he thought I was a dream, and that he did not believe his eyes." The chief led Champlain and his men to his village, which lay on an island nearby (probably the one now known as Morrison), and honored them with a lavish feast. When the feasting had concluded, Champlain asked Tessoüat if he would lend him a few canoes and guides to lead him to the country of the Nipissings (on the border of Lake Nipissing) or even to the "Northern Sea" beyond. What Champlain did not understand was that the Algonquins wished to maintain their position as middlemen in the fur trade—they charged tribute of the Hurons when they passed through their territory on the way to Lachine with furs—and would thus inevitably try to prevent the French from going upriver to meet directly with the Hurons. Upon Tessoüat's objections—the chief cited the difficulty of the route and the hostility of the Nipissings, who were feared as powerful sorcerers—Champlain countered with the experience of Vignau, who claimed to have traveled without any problem through the very country Tessoüat was describing. On hearing this, the assembled Indians turned on Vignau and furiously accused him of not telling the truth. The young Frenchman, they angrily asserted, had never even left their village. Champlain soon concluded that the Indians were telling the truth and that Vignau was nothing more than an "impudent liar."

Opposed by the Indians and unable to rely on Vignau's assurances of a short journey to the northern sea, Champlain was forced to turn back; he had traveled just 175 miles up the Ottawa. He was back at Lachine by June 17. Though he had failed to reach his destination, his expedition had not been fruitless, for by firsthand experience he had added to his own—and France's—store of geographical knowledge about the New World.

After briefly visiting Quebec, whose inhabitants had wintered well, Champlain returned to France, where he hoped to bring to an end the long-standing hostility of a group of Saint-Malo merchants, who claimed that Cartier's discoveries entitled them to the monopoly Champlain's company enjoyed. After arriving at Saint-Malo on September 26, 1613, he convinced, after much negotiation, the most prominent merchants of that town, Rouen, and La Rochelle to join forces with him. On November 20, 1613, a new society called La Compagnie de Canada was formed.

Champlain realized that more than a new business arrangement was needed if New France was to fulfill its potential as a colony. France's European rivals were making considerable progress in establishing New World empires, and their success threatened the security of the still-struggling French colony. The English had been established at Jamestown, Virginia, since 1607 and in 1613 had sent out Sir Samuel Argall to destroy French settlements in Acadia. The Puritans were soon to settle in large numbers in New England, which France claimed as part of Acadia, and the Dutch were getting ready to establish a trading post at what

SAUVAGE NEPISINGUE EN CANADA 1717.

An 18th-century French illustration of a Nipissing warrior. The Nipissings were trading partners of the Hurons, who called them the Nebecerini, or Wizard Nation, because of the supposed power of their sorcerers.

The French missionary tradition in North America began with Champlain. Seen here is a detail from a 1657 map of New France that shows a converted Huron couple praying. Though many of the missionaries were motivated by charitable intentions, they effectively acted as agents of cultural disintegration and were often the unwitting spreaders of the communicable diseases that ravaged the Indian populations.

is now Albany in New York State. The colony at Quebec was still very small, and should it be overrun France might very well be driven out of North America.

One way to widen the French sphere of influence, Champlain recognized, was to send out missionaries to proselytize among the Indians and convert them to Catholicism. Accordingly, he visited a Récollet monastery in his native town of Brouage and selected three friars and one lay brother to return with him to Canada. The four Récollets sailed with Champlain from Honfleur on April 24, 1615; upon arrival at Tadoussac one month later, one of the priests, Père Joseph Le Caron, was so eager to begin his work that he left without delay to winter with the Hurons.

Champlain's business, meanwhile, was warfare, not salvation: His Huron, Algonquin, and Montagnais allies expected him to join them in another campaign against the Iroquois. This new campaign against their enemies would provide the impetus for Champlain's greatest voyage of exploration. Wishing to maintain good relations with these nations, and being eager to visit Huronia, he soon agreed to join in the attack. On July 9, 1615, he set out from Montreal Island for the homeland of the Hurons, ostensibly to recruit warriors to fight the Iroquois. He was accompanied by Étienne Brûlé, one other Frenchman, and 10 Indians.

Traveling in two canoes, this party made rapid progress up the Ottawa and the network of lakes to Lower Allumette Lake. The presence of expert native steersmen and more men to carry equipment made this leg of the journey far easier than it had been in 1613, but beyond Allumette Lake travel became more difficult. For some 75 miles farther up the Ottawa, waterfalls and rapids slowed their progress. The surrounding countryside, Champlain felt, was "far from attractive"; it was quite rocky and struck him as "very barren and sterile" even though covered with pines, birches, and some oaks. It did have one redeeming feature, however; according to Champlain, "God has been pleased to give to these forbidding and desert lands some things in their season for the refreshment of man and the inhabitants of these places. For I assure you that there are along the rivers many strawberries, also a marvellous quantity of blueberries, a little fruit very good to eat, and other small fruits."

On reaching the confluence of the Ottawa and the Mattawa, Champlain's party headed west up the Mattawa and after passing 10 rapids arrived at Lake Nipissing on July 26. Here, the scenery was much more to Champlain's liking; the lake, he noted, was dotted with "pleasant islands" on which one found "fine ponds. . . and meadows" and surrounded by "very fine woods . . . contain[ing] an abundance of game." The northern side of the lake, with its "fine meadows for the grazing of cattle, and many little streams," Champlain found particularly pleasant.

After resting for two days among the Nipissings, who gave the French "a very welcome reception," Champlain's party crossed the lake to the west and entered the French

River, whose course they followed to a vast, island-studded expanse of water—the Georgian Bay of Lake Huron. Champlain had just pioneered the basic route west that would be used by the fur traders of Canada for more than the next 200 years. He called Lake Huron, which the Hochelagans had described to Cartier in 1535, the *Mer douce*, or "Freshwater Sea."

Champlain and his men then took their canoes along the eastern shore of Georgian Bay, through the maze of tiny bodies of land and channels known today as the Thirty Thousand Islands. Four days' travel brought them 100 miles to the Midland Peninsula, where, near the site of present-day Penetanguishene, Ontario, they went ashore. Champlain had reached Huronia, the homeland of the Hurons. Approximately 800 square miles in area, located between Lake Simcoe and Georgian Bay, Huronia was then home to an estimated 10,000 Hurons and was a major entrepôt of the Native Americans' trade network.

On August 1, Champlain's party arrived at a Huron village called Otoüacha. The country thereabouts, wrote Champlain, was "very fine, the largest part being cleared up [i.e, cleared of forest], and several rivers rendering the region agreeable. . . . These localities seemed to me very pleasant, in comparison with so disagreeable a region as that from which we had come." After inspecting the local cornfield, Champlain set out and began walking from village to village gathering troops for the planned campaign against the Iroquois. "It is a pleasure to travel in this country," Champlain remarked, "so fair and fertile it is."

Around August 4, Champlain arrived at a fortified village called Carhouga, located on Midland Peninsula about two miles inland from Thunder Bay. Here he met up with Père Joseph Le Caron, who was greatly surprised to see Champlain in that part of the country. Though in good health, Le Caron had not had much success in converting the local Indians. As he had not yet mastered the language, the Hurons derived great amusement from telling him the

wrong words for things; his sermons thereby were laced with unintentional obscenities and became the object of general hilarity.

Before setting off from Montreal, Champlain had arranged with his allies to rendezvous at Cahiagué, the principal Huron village, located near the present-day town of Hawkestone on Lake Simcoe. His company augmented by eight of the Frenchmen who had accompanied Le Caron, he arrived at Cahiagué on August 17, 1615, and was, he wrote, "received with great joy and gladness by all the savages of the country, who had abandoned their undertaking, in the belief that they would see me no more, and that the Iroquois had captured me." Further cause for rejoicing was provided by the news that the Andastes, allies of the Hurons who lived to the south of the Iroquois, on the

The Iroquois were notably more resistant to the proselytizing efforts of the French than many other tribes. This illustration from a 1664 history of Canada depicts the deaths of the seven French Jesuit missionaries to the Iroquois known collectively as the North American Martyrs.

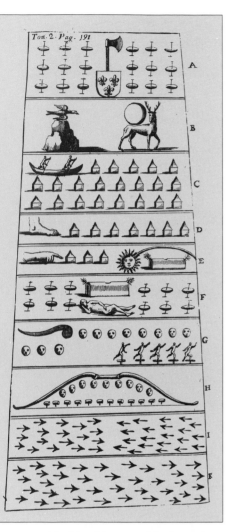

The Five Nations of the Iroquois were extremely sophisticated politically and militarily; to Champlain and his successors in northeastern North America, they were the most fearsome native inhabitants of the continent. Shown here is a Seneca pictograph, published in France in 1705, that depicts a raid on one of their villages.

Susquehanna River just inside the present-day border of the state of Pennsylvania, were eager to join in the campaign and had offered to provide 500 men.

On September 1, Champlain and the bulk of the war party set out from Cahiagué. The huge fleet of canoes paddled up the Severn River, through Sparrow and Couchitching lakes, to Lake Simcoe, where they halted to await the arrival of the remaining forces. A war council was held, and it was decided that a small party should be dispatched immediately to advise the Andastes of the imminent attack. Champlain thought that if the two parties could be properly coordinated, it might be possible to outflank the Iroquois by mounting a simultaneous offensive. Accordingly, on September 8, a dozen Indians set off; with them, at his own suggestion, went Étienne Brûlé, who was eager to see more unexplored territory.

Two days later, the main war party set off towards Iroquois country. The Indian army was made up of several hundred Hurons, together with some Algonquins and Nipissings; the heavily armed French contingent—reinforced by fresh arrivals—consisted of Champlain and perhaps 20 of his men. From the eastern end of Lake Simcoe, this group paddled upstream and eastward across a chain of lakes to the Trent River, which they followed downstream until it entered the Bay of Quinte, near the northeastern end of Lake Ontario.

There before Champlain's eyes lay a second great inland sea. With the exception of Brûlé, who had proceeded him by several days, Champlain was the first European to see this principal source of the St. Lawrence, which he named Lac Saint-Louis. Beginning on October 5, he and the others began paddling southward across the lake, stopping at various islands along the way. On its south shore, they hid their canoes in the woods and began walking south through present-day Oswego County, New York, which to Champlain seemed "very pleasant and beautiful" country with "an endless amount of game, many vines, fine woods, and a large number of chestnut trees, whose fruit . . . is small, but of good flavor."

But the explorer's appreciation of this natural bounty was tempered by his knowledge that he was now in Iroquois country. On October 10, south of Oneida Lake, they came upon an Iroquois village, probably on Atkins Pond, just east of the present-day town of Perryville. The village was protected on one side by open water and by moats on two other sides and was surrounded by tall palisades, topped with galleries piled high with stones and equipped with waterspouts for putting out fires.

As the Andastes had not yet arrived, Champlain decided that it would be best for his forces to keep hidden until the following day. Even so, the Huron warriors were impatient to do battle, and there were several skirmishes with Iroquois scouting parties before the Hurons, over Champlain's objections, impetuously mounted a full-scale attack. This confrontation was quickly concluded: "Although I only had a few men," Champlain wrote, "yet we showed them what they had never seen or heard before; for, as soon as they saw us and heard the arquebus shots and the balls whizzing in their ears, they withdrew speedily to their fort, carrying the dead and wounded in this charge."

Recognizing that the Iroquois town was too strongly fortified to be taken simply by storming the gates, Champlain, drawing on his knowledge of European siege techniques, proposed to his Indian allies that they build a *cavalier*, or moveable tower, which would enable them to overlook the town's palisades and fire down on its defenders. On October 11, the massive wooden structure was pushed by 200 Hurons right up against the Iroquois palisade. As soon as three or four arquebusiers were stationed on the cavalier, and others, including Champlain himself, were positioned on the other side of the fort, an attack was mounted.

While the French kept up a barrage of gunfire, their Indian allies set fire to piles of wood pushed up against the palisades. But the fires were easily extinguished by the

Iroquois, who, undeterred by the arquebusiers, unleashed such an onslaught of stones and arrows that Champlain's Indian allies rapidly became utterly disorganized. After three hours of battle, the attackers withdrew in defeat to the nearby forest.

Although his side did not incur many casualties, Champlain himself had been wounded twice in the leg and was unable to walk. Nevertheless, he wished to continue the assault against the Iroquois and managed to convince the unwilling Hurons to wait four more days for the arrival of Brûlé and the 500 Andastes, but when the reinforcements failed to appear, Champlain reluctantly retreated. From Brûlé, Champlain later learned that the Andastes, though eager to join in the attack, had spent so many days feasting and dancing and making other ceremonial preparations for war that they had missed their rendezvous. They arrived in front of the Iroquois village just in time to witness the inhabitants' victory celebration, then turned around and went home. In attempting to make his way to Huronia, Brûlé was captured by the Iroquois and tortured before he succeeded in making his escape.

Champlain's retreat from the Iroquois country was slow and humiliating. Unable to walk, he was carried for several days in a basket, "bound and pinioned. . . [like] an infant in its swaddling clothes. . . . I never found myself," he wrote, "in such a *gehenna* [hell] as during this time, for the pain which I suffered in consequence of the wound in my knee was nothing in comparison with that which I endured while I was carried bound and pinioned on the back of one of our savages."

The humiliating defeat of the French and Hurons was to have important historical consequences. It led to a decline in Champlain's prestige and shattered the image of European invincibility. The Iroquois, driven from the St. Lawrence Valley and shut out of the fur trade with the French (they would soon enter into profitable commercial intercourse with the English and the Dutch), had known nothing but failure for half a century; victory over Champlain was for them the turning of the tide, and, greatly emboldened, they rapidly attained the position of dominance they maintained for the next 40 years.

It was Champlain's plan to return to Quebec from Lake Ontario, which he reached on October 27, but it soon became clear that the Hurons were not willing to provide an escort. The Indians intended to keep the French with them as protection against the Iroquois, and Champlain resigned himself to returning to Huronia. On December 23, after a gruelling cross-country trek made necessary by frozen lakes and streams, he arrived at Cahiagué.

A newly healed Champlain made the best of his situation by continuing his explorations of Huronia. With Le Caron, who had still not abandoned his mission, he went in mid-January 1616 to visit the Petuns, or Tobacco In-

Champlain's drawing of the Iroquois village near Oneida Lake where his forces were routed in October 1615 shows the siege device, called a cavalier, *that he fashioned in order to allow his gunners to fire down into the settlement.*

dians, who lived to the west of the Hurons between Lake Huron and the Nottawasaga River. While there, he was greatly intrigued by the buffalo pelts the Indians showed him. The sailor and the priest then traveled to the country of the Andatahouats, who lived southwest of Georgian Bay. Champlain called these Indians the *Cheveux-Relevés* (Tufted-Hairs) for their elaborate, upswept hairstyle, which, he wryly remarked, was "better dressed than that of our courtiers, in spite of their irons [supports to keep the hair up] and refinements." (The Indians called themselves the Outaouais, or Ottawas; hence the name of the river and Canada's future capital city.) The explorer learned also about the Neutrals, who lived north of Lake Erie between Lake Ontario and Lake St. Clair, and gathered much information that added to his understanding of the geography of the Great Lakes.

After the spring thaw, on May 20, 1616, Champlain and a few of the other Frenchmen finally began the trip back to Montreal, guided by a party of Hurons. They reached Lachine at the end of June and Quebec by July 11, where Champlain was received with great joy by the colonists, who had given him up for lost.

Despite the failure of the campaign against the Iroquois, the expedition Champlain had just completed was the most significant contribution to European knowledge of the interior of the continent since Cartier's discovery of the

During his painful retreat from Iroquois country to Huronia, Champlain witnessed one Huron method of deer hunting, which he later sketched. Using clappers and noisemakers, the Indians frightened the deer into a V-shaped trap, where they were slaughtered by hunters hidden at the closed end.

St. Lawrence. He had discovered two vast "inland seas," Lake Huron and Lake Ontario, had traveled widely in Huronia, and had gathered much information about the Great Lake system. The map of his wanderings he published in Paris in the winter of 1616 contained major errors and omissions but nonetheless constituted a major contribution to the geographical knowledge of his time and was exceptionally accurate regarding the lands he had traveled. A steady seller, it subsequently went through five editions.

As fruitful as it had been, the exploratory expedition of 1615 was to be Champlain's last. From that point onward, the safeguarding and development of the colony he had founded was his major preoccupation. He made a couple of quick round-trips to Quebec in 1618 and 1619 and wrote and published his third book, *Voyages and Discoveries Made in New France between 1615 and 1618*. In 1620, Louis XIII, acting in part on the reports regarding the colonization of New France that Champlain had prepared, ordered him to concentrate on the administration of Quebec and prohibited any future explorations. This did not prevent Champlain, who was still deeply curious about the geography of the Great Lakes, from sponsoring expeditions by others. Sometime between 1618 and 1628 (probably in 1623), Étienne Brûlé, charged by Champlain with investigating the Great Lakes to the north and west of points previously reached, set off with a companion named Grenolle to explore the waters west of Georgian Bay. These two made their way along the north shore of Lake Huron toward the Sault Ste. Marie and probably passed into Lake Superior itself. Brûlé in all likelihood also visited the country of the Neutrals, north of Lake Erie, sometime before 1626. In 1634, Jean Nicolet, another of Champlain's so-called young men whom he entrusted with expeditions he could no longer make, crossed the north channel of Lake Huron and visited Lake Michigan and Green Bay.

In 1627, Cardinal Richelieu, the most powerful man in France, reorganized the colonization of New France under the direction of his own company, the Cens Associés (Hundred Associates). Though Richelieu recognized Champlain's ability and kept him on in Canada as his personal associate, the cardinal was unsuccessful in attracting colonists for New France, and the colony continued to languish.

Though he engaged in no further exploration, Champlain's later years were not without drama. In 1628, after war had broken out between France and England, Quebec was besieged by English privateers led by the Kirke brothers. Champlain held out until the following summer, when he was forced to surrender the fort. To his disgust, among the occupying force was none other than his trusted associate Étienne Brûlé, who had treacherously gone over to the enemy. Champlain was taken prisoner and brought to England, but he was quickly freed when his captors learned that an armistice had been declared.

In 1632, Quebec was restored to France by the treaty of St. Germain-en-Laye, and in the following year Champlain, in order to resume his control of the colony, made his final trip across the Atlantic. He was then in his early to mid-sixties and did not have long to live; in October of 1635 he suffered a paralytic stroke. He died on Christmas Day, 1635, in the colony he had founded, which by that time had spread along both shores of the St. Lawrence. According to the future martyr Père Paul Le Jeune, the founder of Quebec received

> a very honorable burial, the funeral procession being formed of the people, the soldiers, the captains and the churchmen. Father Lalement officiated at this burial, and I was charged with the funeral oration, for which I did not lack material. Those whom he left behind have reason to be well satisfied with him; for although he died out of France, his name will not therefore be any less glorious to posterity.

One hundred years after Champlain's death, the Jesuit Père de Charlevoix, author of the first great history of Canada, offered the following summation of the explorer's character:

> M. de Champlain was, beyond contradiction, a man of merit, and may be well called, *The Father of New France*. He had good sense, much penetration, very upright views, and no man was ever more skilled in adopting a course in the most complicated affairs. What all admired most in him was his constancy in following up his enterprise, his firmness in the greatest dangers, a courage proof against the most unforeseen reverses and disappointments, ardent and disinterested patriotism, a heart tender and compassionate for the unhappy, and more attentive to the interests of his friends than his own, a high sense of honour and great probity. His memoirs show that he was not ignorant of

anything that one of his profession should know, and we find in him a faithful and sincere historian, an attentively observant traveler, a judicious writer, a good mathematician and an able mariner.

The priests spoke truly; by 1700, New France, which Champlain had done more than any man to create, stretched from the Labrador Sea to the Gulf of Mexico and from the Atlantic Ocean to the Rocky Mountains. Though

From the humble beginnings made by Champlain along the St. Lawrence, France carved out an immense continental empire, as this map, drawn by Jean-Baptiste-Louis Franquelin in 1688, beautifully illustrates. A view of Quebec, the capital city of New France, is at the lower right.

this empire would not last the century, Canada's French heritage remains a distinctive element of its character and culture, especially in Quebec, a legacy that can be traced directly to Champlain. "No other European colony in America," wrote the eminent historian Samuel Eliot Morison, "is so much the lengthened shadow of one man as Canada is of the valiant, wise, and virtuous Samuel de Champlain."

Further Reading

Bishop, Morris. *Champlain: The Life of Fortitude*. New York: Hippocrene, 1979.

Brown, Warren. *The Search for the Northwest Passage*. New York: Chelsea House, 1991.

Dickason, Olive Patricia. *The Myth of the Savage and the Beginnings of French Colonialism in the Americas*. Edmonton: University of Alberta Press, 1984.

Dionne, N. E. *Champlain: Founder of Quebec, Father of New France*. Toronto: University of Toronto Press, 1963.

Eccles, W. J. *Essays on New France*. New York: Oxford University Press, 1988.

Gough, Barry. *Canada*. Englewood Cliffs, NJ: Prentice Hall, 1975.

Grant, W. L., ed. *Voyages of Samuel de Champlain, 1604–1618*. New York: Barnes & Noble Books, 1959.

Josephy, Alvin M., Jr. *The Indian Heritage of America*. New York: Knopf, 1968.

McNaught, Kenneth. *The Penguin History of Canada*. New York: Penguin Books, 1988.

Morison, Samuel Eliot. *Samuel de Champlain: Father of New France*. Boston: Little, Brown, 1972.

Muise, D. A., ed. *A Reader's Guide to Canadian History, No. 1: Beginnings to Confederation*. Toronto: University of Toronto Press, 1982.

Syme, Ronald. *Champlain of the St. Lawrence*. New York: Morrow, 1974.

Toye, William. *The St. Lawrence River*. New York: Henry Z. Walck, 1959.

Trudel, Marcel. *The Beginnings of New France: 1524–1663*. English translation. Toronto: McClelland and Stewart, 1973.

Wrong, George M. *Rise and Fall of New France*. New York: Hippocrene, 1970.

Chronology

1491	Jacques Cartier born in Saint-Malo sometime between June 7 and December 23
1497–1524	After the discovery of rich fishing grounds off the coast of North America, England and France establish fishing stations around the coast of present-day Newfoundland
1519	Cartier marries Marie Katherine des Granches
1534	Sails from Saint-Malo on April 20 and reaches the coast of Newfoundland on May 10; explores the territory around the Gulf of St. Lawrence and returns to France in September
1535	Cartier's second New World voyage; explores the St. Lawrence River, encounters Native Americans at village of Stadacona, and establishes a fort at the future site of the city of Quebec
1541–43	Sails from Saint-Malo on his final voyage with a crew of released convicts, but his progress up the St. Lawrence is again halted by rapids above Montreal; establishes and then abandons settlement at Charlesbourg Royal
Sept. 1, 1557	Dies in Saint-Malo
c. 1570	Samuel de Champlain is born in Brouage, France
1599–1601	Champlain sails the Caribbean and the South Atlantic and writes an account of his travels
1603	Champlain's first voyage to Canada; gathers much geographical information on the region
1604–7	Explores the Atlantic coastline, creating accurate maps and charts
1608–10	Commands another expedition to Canada and establishes the first permanent European settlement in Canada at present-day Quebec; leads the Hurons and Algonquins in battles against the Iroquois; discovers Lake Champlain; upon his return to France, marries Hélène Boullé

1613	Explores the western territory by canoe, traveling up the Ottawa River
1615	Explores territory west of Quebec along the waterways to the Great Lakes; is wounded in battle against the Iroquois
1620–28	Prohibited from any further expeditions by Louis XIII, Champlain concentrates on governing Quebec and sends Étienne Brûlé and others to investigate territory around the Great Lakes
1629	Champlain taken prisoner and sent to England after Quebec's capture by the English
1632	Quebec returned to France by the Treaty of St. Germain-en-Laye
1635	Champlain dies on December 25 after suffering a paralytic stroke
1763	France surrenders its territory in Canada to England

Index

Picture Credits

Alinari/Art Resource: p. 26; The Bettmann Archive: cover (portraits), pp. 12, 32, 44, 48, 62, 73, 82; Bibliothèque Nationale, Paris: cover (map), p. 29; Collection Viollet, Paris: pp. 33, 57, 89; Gilcrease Museum: p.86; Giraudon/Art Resource: pp. 14, 15, 47, 100, 102–3, 66, 70; Huntington Library, San Marino, CA: pp. 68–69; From *Le Monde de Jacques Cartier*, courtesy of Canadian Consulate, photos by Sarah S. Lewis: pp. 16, 18, 23, 24, 40; Musée Seminaire du Québec, p. 43; Museum of Quebec, photo by Neuville Bazin: p. 52; National Archives of Canada: pp. 17 (C17525), 21 (C99222), 28 (C69710), 30–31 (NMC97952), 51 (C17653), 54 (C6643), 58 (C17159), 61 (C99345), 90 (C71502); National Library of Canada: pp. 36 (NL7090), 39 left (NL15309), 39 right (NL15305), 74 (NL15323), 75 (NL 15312), 77 (8759), 78 (6643), 81 (15318), 97 (NL15320), 98 (NL15321); New York Public Library, Astor, Lenox, and Tilden Foundations: p. 34; Photo by L.T. Burwash, Collection Indian and Northern Affairs, Public Archives of Canada, p. 94 (PA99247); Photo Jean-Loup Charmet, Paris: pp. 65, 72, 93; Photographie Bulloz, Paris: pp. 56, 67,71, 84; Scala/Art Resource: p. 68

Tony Coulter has an M.A. in history from Columbia University. He is the author of *La Salle and the Explorers of the Mississippi* in the Chelsea House WORLD EXPLORERS series. The host of two New York radio programs, he currently resides in Brooklyn, New York.

William H. Goetzmann holds the Jack S. Blanton, Sr., Chair in History at the University of Texas at Austin, where he has taught for many years. The author of numerous works on American history and exploration, he won the 1967 Pulitzer and Parkman prizes for his *Exploration and Empire: The Role of the Explorer and Scientist in the Winning of the American West, 1800–1900*. With his son William N. Goetzmann, he coauthored *The West of the Imagination*, which received the Carr P. Collins Award in 1986 from the Texas Institute of Letters. His documentary television series of the same name received a blue ribbon in the history category at the American Film and Video Festival held in New York City in 1987. A recent work, *New Lands, New Men: America and the Second Great Age of Discovery*, was published in 1986 to much critical acclaim.

Michael Collins served as command module pilot on the *Apollo 11* space mission, which landed his colleagues Neil Armstrong and Buzz Aldrin on the moon. A graduate of the United States Military Academy, Collins was named an astronaut in 1963. In 1966 he piloted the *Gemini 10* mission, during which he became the third American to walk in space. The author of several books on space exploration, Collins was director of the Smithsonian Institution's National Air and Space Museum from 1971 to 1978 and is a recipient of the Presidential Medal of Freedom.